2-99 ✓

D0334618

78887

Wuthering Heights

EMILY BRONTË

Guide written by

John Mahoney

A *Letts* EXPLORE **Literature Guide**

ST. HELENS
COLLEGE

823·9
BRO

90692

SEPT 1998

LIBRARY

First published 1994
Reprinted 1998
This edition revised by Ron Simpson

Letts Educational
Aldine House
Aldine Place
London W12 8AW
0181 740 2266

Text © John Mahoney and Stewart Martin 1994

Self-test questions devised by Claire Wright

Typeset by Jordan Publishing Design

Text design Jonathan Barnard

Text illustrations Hugh Marshall

Cover illustration Ivan Allen

Design © BPP (Letts Educational) Ltd

Acknowledgements
Outline answers are solely the responsibility of the author, and are not supplied
or approved by the Exam Board.

All our rights reserved. No part of this publication may be reproduced, stored
in a retrieval system, or transmitted, in any form or by any means, electronic,
mechanical, photocopying, recording or otherwise, without the prior
permission of Letts Educational.

British Library Cataloguing in Publication Data
A CIP record for this book is available from the British Library

ISBN 1 85758 258 6

Printed and bound in Great Britain

Ashford Colour Press, Gosport, Hampshire

Letts Educational is the trading name of BPP (Letts Educational) Ltd

Contents

Plot synopsis

The narrator, Lockwood, is told the story by Nelly Dean, who is housekeeper at Wuthering Heights.

Heathcliff, a child of uncertain origins, is brought from Liverpool by Mr Earnshaw to live with his family on their farm, Wuthering Heights, on the Yorkshire moors. Accepted by Catherine, Earnshaw's daughter, but rejected by Hindley, his son, Heathcliff lives a wild and free life, roaming the moors with Catherine, with whom he develops an intense relationship. One day they spy through the windows of the local mansion house, Thrushcross Grange, and see Edgar and Isabella, the Linton children. Attacked by the Lintons' dogs, Heathcliff is sent home but Catherine remains there to be looked after.

Catherine is impressed with the lifestyle at the Grange and falls in love with Edgar. She tells Nelly that she could not marry Heathcliff because it would degrade her. Heathcliff overhears this and leaves the Heights, not staying to hear her declare her passionate love for him. Three years pass: Catherine marries Edgar, old Mr and Mrs Linton die and Hindley returns from college with his bride, Frances. She gives birth to a son, Hareton, then dies.

After his wife's death, Hindley takes to drink and gambling. Heathcliff now returns to take revenge on Hindley for the way he used to bully him, and on Edgar for marrying Catherine. Heathcliff moves into Wuthering Heights and helps Hindley to gamble his property away – to Heathcliff. He persuades Isabella, Edgar's sister, to elope with him.

Brought back to Wuthering Heights, Isabella is cruelly mistreated by Heathcliff. She runs away to London, where she gives birth to a son, Linton. Heathcliff now has Hareton and Hindley in his power, and treats the latter brutally until his death. Catherine dies while giving birth to a daughter, Cathy. After some years, Isabella dies and Linton returns to live with his father, Heathcliff, who mistreats him. Heathcliff abducts Cathy from Thrushcross Grange and forces her to marry Linton. Edgar dies. Linton is a sickly youth and dies soon afterwards. But Heathcliff now has the last of the Earnshaws and the Lintons, Hareton and Cathy, in his power, and owns all their property and land.

But Heathcliff's desire for revenge has at last worn itself out. Still passionately in love with Catherine, he wills himself to death so that he may be reunited with her. Hareton and Cathy fall in love and unite the two houses, promising a new moral order for the next generation.

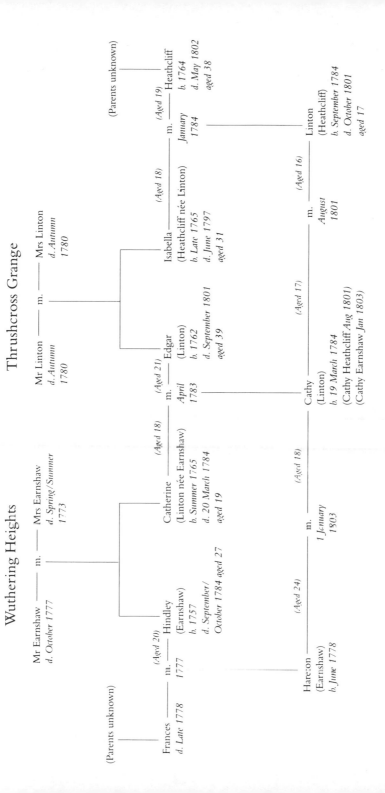

Wuthering Heights

Thrushcross Grange

(Parents unknown)

Mr Earnshaw ——— m. ——— Mrs Earnshaw
d. October 1777   d. Spring/Summer
                                        1773

Mr Linton ——— m. ——— Mrs Linton
d. Autumn   d. Autumn
1780   1780

(Parents unknown)

Frances
d. Late 1778

(Aged 20)
m. ——— Hindley
1777   (Earnshaw)
                 b. 1757
                 d. September/
                 October 1784 aged 27

Catherine
(Linton née Earnshaw)
b. Summer 1765
d. 20 March 1784
aged 19

(Aged 18)

(Aged 21)
m. ——— Edgar
April   (Linton)
1783   b. 1762
                 d. September 1801
                 aged 39

Isabella
(Heathcliff née Linton)
b. Late 1765
d. June 1797
aged 31

(Aged 18)

(Aged 19)
m. ——— Heathcliff
January   b. 1764
1784   d. May 1802
                 aged 38

Hareton
(Earnshaw)
b. June 1778

(Aged 24)

m.
1 January
1803

(Aged 18)

Cathy
(Linton)
b. 19 March 1784
(Cathy Heathcliff Aug 1801)
(Cathy Earnshaw Jan 1803)

(Aged 17)

m.
August
1801

(Aged 16)

Linton
(Heathcliff)
b. September 1784
d. October 1801
aged 17

Heathcliff

Heathcliff's entrance into the novel sets its emotional climate. He is dark-haired and dirty, he is an outsider, and his presence is immediately disruptive. If we examine his role in the novel we see that he is a catalyst; i.e. he changes all the other characters. The narrators (Mr Lockwood and Nelly Dean) try to place him within their accepted sphere of understanding. Nelly sees him as a character in a folk tale; Isabella as a romantic hero; Mr Lockwood as a solitary recluse. Only Catherine understands his energy, determination and ruthless powers of endurance. Animal imagery is used to indicate Heathcliff's violent, savage nature. Later, Catherine tells Isabella 'he's a fierce, pitiless, wolfish man'. After Catherine's death, his desire for revenge destroys the lives of all those around him: 'I have no pity' he says to Nelly in Chapter 14. However, this desire for revenge changes when he sees Catherine's face again at Edgar's burial when the grave is disturbed. After this, he sees her spirit everywhere: 'the entire world is a dreadful collection of memories that she exists and that I have lost her'. When he dies his eyes have 'a frightful, life-like gaze of exultation', and we know that he is reunited with her.

Catherine Earnshaw (Mrs Linton)

Catherine is a spontaneous, natural child: 'her spirits were always at high-water mark, her tongue always going'. Her love for Heathcliff is at the centre of her being: 'she was much too fond of Heathcliff'. She can be imperious: 'in play she liked, exceedingly, to act the little mistress'. In her character as a child are the early signs of later conflict: she thinks she can do as she pleases, and she wants a commanding position in society. When she meets Edgar she thinks she can marry him and continue her relationship with Heathcliff, but Heathcliff regards her marriage as an act of betrayal. She declares to Nelly: 'Nelly, I *am* Heathcliff' and 'Every Linton on the face of the heath might melt into nothing before I would consent to forsake Heathcliff'. She marries Edgar after recovering from the illness brought on by Heathcliff's disappearance. However, as soon as Heathcliff returns she has a breakdown and regresses to childhood: 'the whole last seven years of my life grew a blank'. She dies, and we realise that she never knew what her love for Heathcliff was until he came back and she, by then a mature woman, was unable to accept her loss.

Catherine's diary in Chapter 3 recounts the past in a very effective way. The style is vivid and full of action. We need her first-person account here because it makes us sympathetic towards Catherine and Heathcliff before we read Nelly's account. It introduces her as a living person before we meet her ghost at the end of Chapter 3. The diary gives a vivid picture of the relationship between Catherine and Heathcliff; their rebellion which unites them and their intense love for each other: 'my great miseries in the world have been Heathcliff's miseries'.

Cathy

Cathy Linton (Catherine's daughter)

Cathy is a sweet, biddable little girl: 'that capacity for intense attachments reminded me of her mother' says Nelly Dean, but 'her anger was never furious; her love never fierce, it was deep and tender'. Cathy is important not only because she is Catherine's child, but also as a character in her own right. From her father she inherits greater gentleness, but also an awareness of class and social distinction which can be unpleasant, particularly in her early dealings with Hareton. She becomes less biddable as time passes and when she develops an interest in Wuthering Heights and Linton, she shows her mother's spirit: ' "I can get over the wall" ', she said, laughing. "the Grange is not a prison, Ellen, and you are not my jailer" '. Her love for Linton is maternal: ' "he's a pretty little darling when he's good. I'd make such a pet of him, if he were mine" '. When she is taken to Wuthering Heights and imprisoned there, her resistance to Heathcliff is very brave: ' "if you still use me, Hareton will strike you !" she said, "so you may as well sit down" '. She becomes very embittered when she is at Wuthering

Heights. At first she treats Hareton badly and it is only after Nelly goes there that she tries to make amends: ' "So you won't be my friend?" she said, smiling as sweet as honey, and creeping close up.' However, Hareton and Cathy fall in love and the novel ends with their happiness: 'The red firelight glowed on their two bonny heads, and revealed their faces, animated with the eager interest of children.'

Hindley Earnshaw

In his boyhood, Hindley is jealous of Heathcliff because his father, Mr Earnshaw, favours Heathcliff. When he returns from college with his wife Frances, Hindley torments and degrades Heathcliff, who swears he will get his revenge. When Frances dies, Hindley deteriorates and becomes an alcoholic, giving himself up to reckless dissipation. While he is master, Wuthering Heights becomes a hell for all who live there and words like 'infernal', 'devil' and 'hell' are used to describe him and the house at this time. He becomes so dissipated that he cannot continue his revenge against Heathcliff when he returns to Wuthering Heights. Heathcliff gets the upper hand, lending Hindley money in return for a mortgage on the house. Hindley spends his life making plans to kill Heathcliff, but these are never successful (see Chapter 17). Nelly is aware of Hindley's weak nature, as she says when she compares him with Edgar: 'Hindley, with apparently the stronger head, has shown himself sadly the worse and the weaker man.' Finally, Hindley dies in suspicious circumstances and Joseph is convinced that Heathcliff murdered him. His importance in the novel is firstly that his infantile love for Frances is a contrast to the love of Heathcliff and Catherine, secondly that he is the father of Hareton, and lastly that it is his treatment of the young Heathcliff which sets off Heathcliff's thirst for revenge.

Hareton Earnshaw (Hindley's son)

'On the morning of a fine June day, my first bonny little nursling, and the last of the ancient Earnshaw stock was born'. Hareton is nursed by Nelly until she leaves for Thrushcross Grange when he is five and just learning to read. After this his childhood is a degraded one, with his father ill-treating him, Heathcliff brutalising him and Joseph indulging him. But we realise that, despite all this, there is good in Hareton. Heathcliff, comparing him with Linton, says: 'that Hareton is gold put to the use of paving stones'. When Cathy first comes to Wuthering Heights, she ridicules him and he is deeply upset. He locks Linton and Cathy out of the living room in his jealousy. But slowly, with Nelly's help, Hareton and Cathy come together and fall in love. He helps her rebel against Heathcliff and this unites them, as rebellion also united Catherine and Heathcliff. He feels great affection for Heathcliff and is the only one to mourn his death.

Edgar Linton

Edgar Linton is a complete contrast to Heathcliff. He is a conventional man, interested in books and dependent on a civilised framework of life. He can be inflexible and cruel if anyone steps outside this: for example, he refuses to communicate with his sister Isabella once she has married Heathcliff. We first see him, through the contemptuous eyes of Heathcliff, quarrelling with Isabella. Nelly's description of him is quite fair: 'he wanted spirit in general'. This lack of spirit is shown when he encounters Heathcliff after Catherine locks him in: 'Mr Edgar was taken with a nervous trembling, and his countenance grew deadly pale.' His love endures not, as Heathcliff's does, in passion, but in acceptance: 'Time brought resignation, and a melancholy sweeter than common joy'. He remains at Thrushcross Grange, protecting his daughter Cathy: 'Mr Linton would take her with him, a mile or so outside, on rare occasions, but trusted no one else'. He gradually withdraws from society until his death, which is peaceful: 'I am going to her, and you, darling child, shall come to us.'

Mr Lockwood

Mr Lockwood is a conventional eighteenth-century gentleman. He is dignified and unbending, and his reactions to the extraordinary situations he encounters are a source of humour. Perhaps the two most noticeable things about his character are how little he understands himself or others, and how little he changes during the course of the novel. He fails to comprehend Nelly's story: the events and personalities of *Wuthering Heights* are simply beyond his sphere of understanding. But this makes him an unbiased narrator.

He is a civilised, rather artificial man and his judgements reflect this. However, his curiosity makes him an invaluable narrator. He sees himself as a strong, solitary figure and thinks he recognises a sympathetic nature in Heathcliff. This and other misconceptions on his part have the effect of emphasising to the reader just how strange the world of *Wuthering Heights* is. His narration is similar to Isabella's in that he describes what he sees from a viewpoint which does not fully comprehend what it sees and hears, leaving the reader to come to his or her own conclusions.

Nelly Dean

Although a servant, Nelly is accepted as an equal by the characters in the book. She has much common sense and this inspires people to confide in her. Another servant, Zillah, refers to her as: 'cant Nelly Dean' (cant is a dialect word which means brisk). She is dependable, and epitomises the Yorkshire spirit of endurance which Lockwood discerns: 'people in these regions so live more in earnest, more in themselves, and less in surface change and frivolous external things.' She esteems herself 'a steady reasonable kind of lady.' Physically she is 'stout and soon put out of breath.' All these qualities commend her as a reliable narrator, but she does show faulty judgement sometimes. For example, she tells Edgar about Heathcliff's attentions to Isabella when it would have been better only to tell Catherine. She is too indulgent to Cathy and underestimates Heathcliff's ruthlessness, but she is a credible character and we respect her integrity.

Linton Heathcliff (Heathcliff's son)

Linton is described by Nelly as 'the worst tempered bit of a sickly slip that ever struggled into his teens!' He is an invalid, and his major characterisitics are spite and pettiness, except for one occasion when he speaks seriously to Cathy in Chapter 24. Heathcliff's contempt for Linton makes him feel worthless, and he directs his bitterness and anger at everybody else. He feels trapped by his own personality and, as his physical condition deteriorates, it is only his fear of Heathcliff's rage which forces him to act. When he has married Cathy he becomes passive and childish, echoing his father's words and ceasing to take even minimal responsibility.

Isabella (Mrs Heathcliff)

Isabella's character is not well developed in the novel. In many ways, she remains a child. We first see her squabbling with Edgar in Chapter 6. She immediately cries when Heathcliff attacks her brother. When Catherine moves to Thrushcross Grange, Isabella is 'a charming young lady of eighteen; infantile in manners, though possessed of keen wit, keen feelings and a keen temper too'. Isabella sees her love for Heathcliff as a grand passion and dislikes Nelly for criticising him. Her love for Heathcliff is dramatic and exaggerated; she has little sense of reality. When Heathcliff rejects her after their marriage, her love turns rapidly to hatred: 'He's a lying fiend, a monster and not a human being!… The single pleasure I can imagine is to die, or to see him dead!'

Joseph

Joseph is cantankerous and bound by an over-strict view of religion, almost incapable of seeing good in others, though he is capable of loyalty, to place as much as to people: he will be the only one to remain at Wuthering Heights when Hareton and Cathy marry. He is there, usually in the background, for the full duration of the novel and suggests the bleak harshness of the world of the Heights even before evil and madness enter. The representation of Yorkshire dialect in his speech at first appears impenetrable, but is in fact consistent and convincing. It is also interesting to consider how far we are intended to see Joseph as a comic figure.

Themes and images in *Wuthering Heights*

Love and passion

Love and passion

Love, in tandem with hate, is the main theme of the novel, but there are many different kinds of love. The love of Heathcliff and Catherine turns to passion, but in childhood it was a selfless love. When Catherine tells Nelly 'I *am* Heathcliff' she describes their other-worldly union. The symbols Catherine uses to describe their love – fire and earth – are elemental and enduring. It is only later, when she ruins their union by marrying Edgar, that their love becomes destructive.

Edgar's love for Catherine is mild by comparision, though his affection for her is genuine. Catherine's love for Edgar is based on desire for social importance and for the ease and grace of life at Thrushcross Grange. Hindley's love for Frances is over-indulgent and her love for him childish and unrealistic.

The love of Isabella for Heathcliff is an unnatural obsession, excited by her reading of romantic fiction. Linton's love for Cathy is that of a baby for its mother: dependent, desiring protection. She responds with an almost maternal love. In contrast to all these kinds of love, that between Hareton and Cathy is positive, balanced, adult and life-giving. It is important to see that both these characters gave love to those around them throughout their childhood: Cathy loved her father and Nelly Dean, whilst Hareton loved Heathcliff.

Passion is shown to be uncontrolled and destructive, the result of frustrated love. The passion of Heathcliff and Catherine, reunited after three years apart, is very different from their earlier love.

Windows and eyes

Windows and eyes

Windows are important images in the novel, used to let people see into worlds which they never knew existed. In Chapter 6, Catherine and Heathcliff look through a window of Thrushcross Grange and are amazed at the luxury within. In Chapter 10, Catherine and Linton look out at the wild moor through a window of the Grange, just before Heathcliff (in many ways a child of the moor) arrives. The windows at Wuthering Heights are small and, when Heathcliff turns it into a prison, they are barred. In Chapter 3, Lockwood's encounter with Catherine's ghost is through a window whose 'hook was soldered into the staple'. Eyes are often described as windows and at one point a comparison is drawn between Heathcliff's eyes and the fortified windows of Wuthering Heights.

Nature

Nature and associated images

The moor is connected with wildness and freedom. It is here that Catherine and Heathcliff roam free as children, and they are buried together on the moors. The moors represent Catherine's idea of heaven.

The moors are important because they bring out the elemental, enduring quality of Heathcliff. Nelly describes him as: 'hard as whinstone' in Chapter 4 and Catherine echoes her in Chapter 10. In Chapter 8, Nelly uses earth imagery to contrast Edgar and Heathcliff: Heathcliff is described as 'bleak, hilly coal country' and Edgar as 'a beautiful fertile valley'. Catherine's description of Heathcliff in Chapter 9 is important. It emphasises the enduring quality of their love compared to her ephemeral love for Edgar: 'My love for Linton is like the foliage in the woods. Time will change it… My love for Heathcliff resembles the eternal rocks beneath…'

Descriptions of the weather are important in *Wuthering Heights*. They symbolise feelings and actions in the novel. Storms signal danger and conflict: when Heathcliff disappears, a tree is struck by lightning; there is a storm the night Catherine is buried. As Cathy grows up, descriptions of calm, summery weather become more frequent.

Imprisonment

Imprisonment

Imprisonment takes many forms in the novel. The physical imprisonment of people is a way of wielding power, an attempt to deprive people of freedom in a mental as well as physical sense. Heathcliff imprisons Cathy at the Heights to punish her for running away. Ironically, it is her desire for freedom from Thrushcross Grange which leads to a much worse imprisonment at the Heights. People may be imprisoned for a short time because of anger: Catherine locks Edgar in the same room as Heathcliff; Hareton locks Cathy and Linton out of the living room. Another form of imprisonment is one which springs from care and concern: Edgar is overprotective of Cathy and will not let her leave Thrushcross Grange. There is also self-imprisonment in an emotional sense. Heathcliff *has* to come back to Wuthering Heights in case Catherine is there; Edgar cannot leave Thrushcross Grange because of his grief for Catherine; Linton feels imprisoned by his own miserable character. Heathcliff's obsession for revenge is also a kind of imprisonment. Only by dying does he become free of it, freeing Cathy and Hareton at the same time.

Books

Books

Books are connected with Catherine, Joseph, Edgar, Linton, Isabella, Cathy, and Hareton. The way in which each uses books shows aspects of character. Catherine uses books as an outflow for her creativity: she writes in them but doesn't appear to read them. Joseph uses books, Calvinist tracts on sin and damnation, as an extension of his puritanical delight in spoiling others' pleasure. Edgar uses books to escape reality: Catherine is scornful of his ability to read them when he should be concerned about her health. Isabella's liking for romantic and Gothic fiction causes her to romanticise her infatuation with Heathcliff. Cathy reads books for entertainment when she is imprisoned at Thrushcross Grange or Wuthering Heights. For Linton, books are a diversion. To Hareton, who was just learning to read at five but then learned no more until he was twenty-three, books are precious objects which hold the key to civilisation and social advancement.

Childhood

The childhood of Catherine and Heathcliff is wild and free. It is a time when their love is not marred by any conflict: they are united against Hindley and Joseph. They spend a lot of time together on the moors. This is the time to which Catherine returns in her mind (Chapters 14 and 15) when she breaks down under stress. Their childhood contrasts with Hareton's, which is isolated and degraded; Cathy's, which is overprotected and unrealistic; and Linton's, which is one of ill health and self-hatred.

Death

Death is a recurring theme in the novel. The novel is set in an age when the mortality rate was high and death was therefore a part of everyday life. In the novel, the death of a character has an effect on others and is often a significant point in the story. For example, Mr Earnshaw's death brings Hindley back to Wuthering Heights and this sets the cycle of revenge in motion. As a result of her father's death, Cathy is forced to leave Thrushcross Grange and become a prisoner at Wuthering Heights. Hindley's death deprives Hareton of his inheritance and it is not until the death of Heathcliff that he regains it.

Folk tale

In her description of Heathcliff's background, Nelly speaks as if she is recounting a folk tale (see Chapter 7). This theme is also evident in the description of Mr Earnshaw's journey, Nelly's songs, the ghost-tale element of the graves in Chapter 29, and Heathcliff's burial. There is also an element of folk tale in the description of Thrushcross Grange when Cathy is growing up: the princess waits for her prince in isolation from the outside world. Wuthering Heights is a grim fortress and in a happy ending, Cathy and Hareton are married on New Year's Day.

Narrators

In this novel, there is no all-knowing narrator. The story is told by various characters involved in it. By using this method of multi-narration, Emily Brontë gives an objective, full account which is extremely vivid, as it is based on first-hand experience. Each narrator has an individual viewpoint and we can judge and select what we consider to be the truth. An important result of Brontë's multi-narration technique is the ease with which the action moves from past to present. The narration returns to the present when we need breathing-space to think about what we have learned, or when we need to see a character from another viewpoint.

The outsider

Both Heathcliff and Mr Lockwood are strangers to the worlds they enter.

Heathcliff's persona is out of sympathy with the world he encounters and his presence causes conflict within it. He first appears as a waif whose origins nobody knows (Chapter 4) and he immediately divides the household. When he returns to Thrushcross Grange (Chapter 10) he aggravates Edgar and torments Catherine. From then on, his obsession with revenge disrupts everything. At his death, peace returns.

The fact that Lockwood comes from outside the society of Wuthering Heights sometimes makes his comments unintentionally comic.

In a way, Linton, Heathcliff's son, is also an outsider. His arrival at Wuthering Heights after his mother's death allows for the three-way conflict between himself, Cathy and Hareton, which mirrors the earlier one between Heathcliff, Catherine and Edgar.

Essays/Examiner's tip icon

This icon is used to draw attention to a section of the **Text commentary** that is particularly relevant to either the section on **How to write a coursework essay** or to the section on **How to write an examination essay**. Each time it is used, a note identifies which section it relates to and adds a comment, quotation or piece of advice.

■ Text commentary

The time sequence in the novel is very meticulous: everything is carefully planned to fit an overall timescale. As you read the novel, notice that the first paragraph of each chapter ties events to the timescale of the action.

The story begins in November 1801. The first three chapters tell us of three days in that month. Then the history of the families is related from Chapters 4–30, which bring us back to the same period, ending at the end of 1802. This device gives the story the quality of an exciting adventure tale. We are plunged into the middle of events, our curiosity is aroused with Lockwood's, and we read to learn more, just as he questions Nelly to find out more. We gradually learn about the characters and events and because they are narrated from more than one point of view, we are free to make up our own minds about them.

Chapter 1

Mr Lockwood describes his first visit to Wuthering Heights. The place and its inhabitants are very unfriendly, but being 'romantically' inclined, he sees Heathcliff as a man similar to himself, a taciturn recluse: he is wrong about Heathcliff, and about himself! He is determined to pay another visit to the Heights the next day.

Mr Lockwood visits his landlord

Mr Lockwood is the narrator of the first part of the novel, recording the events in his diary, dated 1801. He is the new tenant of Thrushcross Grange, which he has rented in order to enjoy peace and quiet and to recover from an 'unhappy love affair'. Because he comes from 'civilised society', a man we can 'recognise', his narration of the extraordinary events of the book makes them more believable and we trust him to tell the truth – as he sees it.

Narration

Lockwood's credentials as a narrator are instantly apparent. Whilst completely honest, he misunderstands the world of Wuthering Heights and Heathcliff ('a capital fellow!'). The result: an increased sense of mystery and strangeness in 'a situation so completely removed from the stir of society'.

At the same time as telling the truth, Lockwood often misunderstands it. His account of the 'most fascinating creature' he met on the coast is mannered and affected and he succeeds in misunderstanding nearly every character and situation at Wuthering Heights. This can be heartlessly amusing, but it helps to suggest the strangeness of Heathcliff's world and also invites the reader to interpret events for him(her)self.

His landlord, Heathcliff, does not extend him a friendly welcome. His surliness, the chained gate, the few 'stunted firs', 'gaunt thorns', and the 'narrow windows' of the house create a chilling and unwelcoming atmosphere. It is worth noting that just as the trees are distorted by the physical climate of the place, the behaviour of the inhabitants is distorted by the emotional climate. The name of the place reflects its situation and climate: 'wuthering' is a dialect word for stormy.

Nature

> **Place**
> Wuthering Heights' character is apparent: 'the narrow windows are deeply set in the walls and the corners defended with large jutting stones'. Note, too, the links with tradition and family history: 'Hareton Earnshaw, 1500'.

'A capital fellow'

That Heathcliff does not merge with his surroundings and is, indeed, 'in singular contrast' should alert us to a mystery that surrounds him – where does he come from? Lockwood recognises Heathcliff as being like himself, calling him 'exaggeratedly reserved' and a 'capital fellow'. However, Heathcliff is completely unlike any person Lockwood has ever before met.

Chapter 2

Lockwood's second visit is equally unsuccessful. He meets (and misunderstands the relationship between) Cathy, Hareton and Heathcliff. The savage nature of the inhabitants (humans and animals) persuades him to leave, but by that time he finds he is snowed in and is forced to stay the night.

The inhabitants of the Heights

On his second visit, Mr Lockwood finds the hostility of Wuthering Heights

is reinforced by the bleak weather and by the isolated nature of its location. Note, however, that while the fires are out at Thrushcross Grange (which decides Lockwood on going out), 'an immense fire' is going in 'the huge, warm, cheerful apartment' at the Heights. This serves as a homely contrast to the strange behaviour of its inhabitants.

Windows and eyes

Mr Lockwood meets Cathy and Hareton. Both are described in detail. He says that Cathy stares at him – notice how much character Brontë attributes to her eyes: 'scorn and a kind of desperation'. Eyes are indicative of personality throughout the novel. In Chapter 15, before Heathcliff and Catherine part for ever, Heathcliff says: 'Kiss me again; and don't let me see your eyes!'

Mr Lockwood discovers some rabbits

Mr Lockwood's efforts to make conversation with Cathy are unsuccessful, and when he mistakes a heap of dead rabbits for a cushion full of cats we are aware of the ironic humour. We also see Lockwood's fallibility as an observer (and therefore narrator): he gets both Cathy's and Hareton's identities wrong – twice. After exhaustive questioning of a surly and uncommunicative Heathcliff, who mocks him for venturing out in such bad weather, he discovers that the young woman is Cathy Heathcliff, his dead son's widow, and that Hareton is Hareton Earnshaw.

Mr Lockwood is startled by the hatred Heathcliff has for Cathy. Joseph fears her because he believes that she has supernatural powers – a suspicion she tauntingly encourages. This exchange prepares us for our encounter with Catherine's ghost. Note the background of religious zealotry and superstition which forms a contrast to the wild and natural 'religion' of Catherine and Heathcliff.

Mr Heathcliff reacts to Lockwood

Imprisonment

Mr Heathcliff's behaviour is more extreme on this occasion and he loses his temper at Mr Lockwood's tactless questions. His rude aggression is heightened by the savage ferocity of the dogs which attack Mr Lockwood when he tries to leave. However, Cathy and Hareton show him some human kindness. We are also aware that the reason the house is barred and bolted is so that Cathy cannot get out. We have to go to Chapter 29 to find out the cause. This is just one of several unanswered questions which intrigue the reader in the first two chapters.

Chased by dogs, his nose bleeding, and finally having a pail of icy water thrown over him, Lockwood cuts the figure of a comic buffoon: no wonder Heathcliff and Hareton laugh. The physical violence prepares us for the emotional storms we are to meet in the next chapter.

Chapter 3

Lockwood is shown to a room with the bed in a cupboard-like alcove next to the window. There he discovers diaries written years before by Catherine Earnshaw. They tell of events at Wuthering Heights just after Mr Earnshaw's death. Lockwood eventually gets to sleep but suffers terrible dreams. It is at this point that he encounters Catherine's ghost; she grips his hand and, in an attempt to get free, he saws her hand to and fro across the glass of the broken window. His cries arouse Heathcliff who, discovering what has happened, calls out after the ghost in anguish. The next day Lockwood returns to Thrushcross Grange.

Catherine Earnshaw's diary

Zillah shows Mr Lockwood to a room which contains a box-bed. On the window-ledge of this he sees the names 'Catherine Earnshaw', 'Catherine Heathcliff' and 'Catherine Linton' scratched. Lockwood examines a Testament on the window-ledge. The name Catherine Earnshaw is written on the fly-leaf, and he opens it to find a diary, written wherever there is space, dating from twenty-five years before.

The diary records the events of a dismal Sunday in the lives of Heathcliff and Catherine, who are being victimised by Hindley, his wife Frances and the god-fearing Joseph. The love between Hindley and Frances is shown to be infantile in comparison with the depth of feeling between Heathcliff and Catherine. The last two rebel against their treatment, refusing to read the good books offered by Joseph. It is obvious why Catherine uses these books to write in – she has little respect for their contents.

Eventually, Catherine and Heathcliff escape to the moors together, as they have been banished from the fire in the living room to Joseph's domain in the back kitchen. Hindley punishes them for this: he appears to be exacting revenge on Heathcliff because he was Mr Earnshaw's favourite.

Mr Lockwood's dream

Mr Lockwood looks at another of the books and then falls asleep. He has a nightmare in which he dreams he is travelling over the moor and has come to Gimmerton Kirk, where he has to listen to a sermon against which he rebels.

All the events in the dream sequence have their origin in his violent experiences the evening before. Startled, he wakes, then dozes again. This time he dreams he hears a noise at the window. Opening it, he clasps a small, cold hand and a voice implores him to let her in. The ghost is that of Catherine Linton; she says she has wanted to come in for twenty years. Horrified, he tries to break her grip by sawing it to and fro on the broken glass: her blood runs on to the bedclothes.

Mr Lockwood's shouts bring Heathcliff into the bedroom. The fact that the narrator is overwrought makes this scene emotional and intense. We

---

Place

The memory of the events of the story is a part of Wuthering Heights. Note that the mysterious (the house haunted by a tormented Catherine) and the ordinary (her daughter reading by the fire) exist side by side. Note also the inaccessibility (Lockwood's tortured walk home).

Love and passion

know, when we have read the novel, that Heathcliff sees his love as lasting beyond death and longs to have a sign that Catherine remembers him. (Catherine, too, believes that she will pursue Heathcliff from the grave until he joins her: see Chapter 12.) His anguished words: 'Hear me this time – Catherine, at last!' reveal that Heathcliff has often implored her ghost to appear before him.

Wuthering Heights – a prison and a place of warmth

Books

Mr Lockwood goes to the living room where he sees Cathy Heathcliff at the fire. Her liking for the fire (remember her mother Catherine's love of the fire) and the fact that she is reading are part of the symbolic framework of the novel. Catherine's treatment of books is very different from her daughter's: the elder Catherine wrote in them, whilst the younger reads them. Joseph uses religious books to tyrannise the children. Later, we see that Edgar Linton seems to retreat into his books to avoid emotional scenes (Chapter 11). The fire at Wuthering Heights is a life-giving force and underlines the ambivalence in the house, which can be full of life and warmth, or a prison which degrades and brutalises its inhabitants.

How many Catherines?

Note that in this chapter we have 'met' Catherine Earnshaw (the diary writer), Catherine Linton (the ghost) and Catherine Heathcliff (in the present-day Wuthering Heights) – the three names inscribed on the window-ledge. Later in the novel we see Catherine Earnshaw marry Edgar to become Catherine Linton – but there is a sense in which she is Catherine Heathcliff (they see themselves almost as one person). Cathy, her daughter, was a Linton, then married a Heathcliff – but will bring the wheel full circle by marrying an Earnshaw.

Examiner's tip

The overlapping of names in the three Catherines hints at the story-lines, choices and possibilities that will present themselves. These three names unite the two halves of the novel, as in the question on page 63. Catherine was (or imagined herself) all three; her daughter will also bear all three, finally returning to her mother's first surname.

Chapter 4

Nelly Dean, Lockwood's housekeeper, is persuaded to begin recounting the history of Wuthering Heights and tells him how Heathcliff was first brought there by old Mr Earnshaw. Heathcliff's arrival split the household: he was Earnshaw's favourite. Mrs Earnshaw dies.

Anothor narrator – Nelly Dean

Mr Lockwood asks Nelly about the people at Wuthering Heights. She gives substance to her credibility and gains acceptance as a narrator by emphasising her long-standing connections with the family, her objective assessment of Heathcliff and her knowledge of the family's history. She begins to narrate the story, and a double narrative begins, with Nelly telling the story and Mr Lockwood recording it. We trust her judgement and are aware of his interest. Her story takes us back to about 1771, thirty years before 1801, and this chapter takes us up to Mr Earnshaw's illness.

Narration

Much of the story will now be told to entertain the ailing Mr Lockwood. Nelly Dean (who needs 'no further invitation to her story') is the ideal narrator: involved in the story, but not as a principal, she is inquisitive, gossipy, on conversational terms with everyone and has a phenomenal memory.

The arrival of Heathcliff at Wuthering Heights

Mr Earnshaw goes on a journey to Liverpool and brings back home 'a dirty,

ragged, black-haired child'. His two children, Hindley and Catherine, are disappointed that they have no presents. Nelly dislikes the stranger, but Catherine becomes very friendly with him. However he appears to have a strange hold over Mr Earnshaw, who favours him over his own children. Hindley becomes jealous of this and sees Heathcliff as a threat.

Heathcliff is determined to get his own way and will suffer any hardships to further his own ends. The chapter ends with Nelly telling Mr Lockwood how wrong she was in thinking Hindley was not vindictive.

Chapter 5

Hindley goes to college. Heathcliff and Catherine develop an intense relationship. Mr Earnshaw dies.

Death, disease and heaven

Mr Earnshaw's health deteriorates. Disease is a recurrent theme in the novel:

Hindley becomes an alcoholic and dies violently in madness; Frances dies of consumption, as does Linton; Catherine dies in childbirth with her reason impaired. These deaths affect the behaviour of other characters.

Catherine grows up a wild girl, rebellious of authority and passionately fond of Heathcliff. Her idea of heaven, which she speaks about in Chapter 9, is the complete freedom of the moors, not the conventional idea of heaven.

The contradictions in Catherine's nature are well illustrated in the death of her father. Her quiet and gentleness are untypical, she cannot resist a sharp retort to the dying man, but she is affectionate, kisses him, sings to him and is grief-stricken at his death.

Mr Earnshaw's death heralds the break-up of the traditional way of life at Wuthering Heights.

Chapter 6

Hindley returns to Wuthering Heights with a bride, Frances. Heathcliff narrates his and Catherine's visit to Thrushcross Grange. They see the two Linton children, Isabella and Edgar, through the windows, but are not impressed by their cosseted lives. Catherine is bitten by the Lintons' dog and stays there while she recovers. Heathcliff returns to Wuthering Heights.

Hindley returns with a bride

Hindley returns, bringing his bride, Frances, with him. He makes a distinction between his wife and himself, and the rest of the inhabitants of the Heights. Heathcliff and Catherine rebel against his degrading treatment of them and Joseph's tyranny: they escape to the freedom of the moors.

Heathcliff narrates the Thrushcross Grange visit

Catherine and Heathcliff go to Thrushcross Grange and Heathcliff tells Nelly

what has happened. He is a good narrator because he is an outsider to the world of civilisation, so his comments are all the more effective. Heathcliff's method of speaking, direct and full of energy, is indicative of his passionate nature and determination. This is the first time he has spoken directly about his feelings and we realise the depth of his love for

Heathcliff

Catherine. He tells Nelly how he and Catherine looked through the window at Thrushcross Grange and saw the young Lintons, Isabella and Edgar, quarrelling over a little dog.

Place
Thrushcross Grange symbolises the comfortable life of the protected Lintons: 'a splendid place carpeted with crimson...' Once again Brontë makes a perfect choice of **Narrator**: Heathcliff, astonished, impressed and not a little resentful.

Edgar and Isabella appear to have a conventional affection for each other. (We will see later how Edgar is cold towards her when she marries Heathcliff,

23

refusing to see her or help her.) They are disturbed by the intruders at the window and the servants set the dogs on Heathcliff and Catherine. At first they are taken for thieves, but then Catherine is recognised as Miss Earnshaw and Heathcliff as the 'strange acquisition from Liverpool'. Heathcliff is turned out but Catherine stays; she is delighted when they treat her as a young lady.

Heathcliff is not at all envious of Catherine's fortune, commenting only on the Lintons' 'stupid admiration' for her. After this visit to the Grange, the relationship between Heathcliff and Catherine changes: she has glimpsed a lifestyle to which she aspires, one which he holds in contempt.

Chapter 7

Catherine returns home after five weeks, delighted with her new friends. The Lintons visit, and Heathcliff comes into conflict with Edgar. This results in Heathcliff being flogged and locked up.

Catherine returns

When Catherine returns to Wuthering Heights she is elegantly dressed, and the contrast between her civilised appearance and Heathcliff's unwashed savagery is emphasised.

Hindley orders Heathcliff to the garret when the Lintons visit the Grange, although Nelly protests at Hindley's unfairness. Edgar makes an insolent remark and Heathcliff hurls a tureen of apple sauce at him. Catherine takes Heathcliff's side against Edgar. The visit is ruined for her because of the way Heathcliff has been treated.

The conflict between Heathcliff and Edgar over Catherine begins

Though Catherine wants to impress Edgar, her loyalties are with Heathcliff; the seeds of their later conflict are evident here. Heathcliff tells Nelly of his desire for revenge on Hindley. Nelly tells him that revenge is a matter for God. Notice that Heathcliff has no sense of Christian forgiveness: 'God won't have the satisfaction that I shall'. At the end of the chapter we move back into the present. Lockwood praises Nelly for the intelligence and objectivity of her narration.

The pause in narration reminds us that what we are reading is history and provides a respite before the next series of events.

■ Self-test questions Chapters 1–7

Uncover the plot

Delete two of the three alternatives given, to find the correct plot. Beware possible misconceptions and muddles.

Lockwood/Dean/Heathcliff, tenant of Thrushcross Heights/Farm/Grange, visits Earnshaw/Linton/Heathcliff, finding him welcoming/inhospitable/sinister, and meets Mrs Linton/Earnshaw/Heathcliff, sickly/timid/scornful widow of Hareton's/ Heathcliff's/Earnshaw's son, and Hareton/Hindley/Linton Earnshaw: both seem hated/ loved/ignored by Heathcliff. Lockwood reads Frances'/Catherine's/Isabella's diary of Heathcliff's/Hareton's/ Hindley's cruelty and dreams of Catherine Linton's/ Earnshaw's/Heathcliff's ghost. Mrs Zillah/Dean/Linton says Heathcliff, found by Mr Linton/Earnshaw/Heathcliff, was 'thick' with Nelly/Hindley/Catherine, but ill-treated by Edgar/Hindley/Hareton, who returned from college/prison/the Grange with Isabella/Frances/Ellen when Mr Linton/Earnshaw/Heathcliff died. Heathcliff and Hareton/Catherine/Edgar ran wild: at the Heights/church/Grange, Catherine/Edgar/ Heathcliff was injured and fled/stayed/screamed. Attracted to the Lintons/Earnshaws/ Deans, she still felt for Heathcliff, unfairly punished by Hindley/Edgar/Joseph.

Who? What? When? Where? Why? How?

1 Who does Lockwood first think 'Mrs Heathcliff' and Hareton Earnshaw are – and who are they?
2 Whose names are inscribed in the room Lockwood stays in, and why is this significant?
3 What is Lockwood's second dream at Wuthering Heights?
4 What brings about Catherine's link with the Lintons, and what is significant about the incident?
5 When does Heathcliff first meditate revenge against Hindley – and why?
6 Where is Heathcliff from – and why is this significant?
7 Why did Hindley grow bitter as a young man, before being sent away to college?
8 Why does Heathcliff throw apple sauce over Edgar?
9 How is Heathcliff able to bear Hindley's treatment after Mr Earnshaw's death?
10 How does Frances try to 'reform' Catherine after her stay at the Grange?

Once upon a time...

Variations of narrative viewpoint and timescheme are important in the novel. Let's explore...

1 Who is the overall narrator? What are we encouraged to think of his judgements, and why?
2 From whose point of view do we first see Heathcliff's past, through what device – and to what effect?
3 Who gives a chronological narration of past events? What are his/her qualifications as a narrator?
4 Who else is a narrator, how, and of what events?
5 What is the 'present' time? List the 'flashbacks' in these chapters, and when they are set.

Familiar themes

1 Give two examples of (a) locking in and (b) locking out in these chapters.
2 Give an example of the rôle of dogs in these chapters.
3 Give an example of the rôle of windows in these chapters.

4 What is our first view of Thrushcross Grange? How does it contrast with Wuthering Heights here – and later (or earlier) when we 'flashback' to Heathcliff and Cathy's first 'visit'?

5 What is the weather like on the night Lockwood stays at Wuthering Heights? Why is this important?

A capital fellow!

The narrators admit to difficulties fathoming the character of Heathcliff. Let's explore…

1 Mr Lockwood's first impression is that 'Heathcliff forms a singular contrast to his abode'. How?

2 What are the first hints Lockwood picks up of a past relationship between Heathcliff and Catherine?

3 What immediate effect does Heathcliff's arrival as a child have on the other inmates of the Heights?

4 What makes Heathcliff seem 'devilish' – and what counters this impression?

5 How does Nelly compare Heathcliff to Edgar? What differences does Heathcliff see?

Chapter 8

Hareton Earnshaw is born to Hindley and Frances, but Frances dies shortly afterwards. Hindley is devastated and begins to drink heavily, venting his anger on all around him, especially on Heathcliff. Catherine and Edgar realise they are in love.

Hareton is born, Frances dies

Frances gives birth to Hareton but dies of consumption soon after. Hindley rages in grief and becomes so tyrannical that all the servants except Nelly and Joseph leave. Nelly describes the house as 'infernal' and says that Heathcliff had 'something diabolical' about him. The world of Wuthering Heights is becoming a personal hell for its inhabitants. Hindley is distraught with grief, Heathcliff is degraded, and Catherine is torn between her desire for social advancement and her love for Heathcliff.

Catherine and Edgar declare their love

Catherine's show of temper is the result of her guilt at treating Heathcliff badly and her inability to see why she can't love both Heathcliff and Linton. This is the compromise she tries to effect in Chapter 10. When Nelly refuses to leave the kitchen on Edgar's arrival, Catherine slaps her, shakes Hareton, and when Edgar intervenes she boxes his ears. He begins to leave but lacks the strength of will: he returns and in making up their quarrel they declare their love for each other.

Clearly Catherine has great power over the emotions of Heathcliff and Edgar. She drives Heathcliff to 'much agitation' and Edgar is unable to leave even after the humiliation of being struck. How much power does Catherine have over *her own* emotions? Or is she as trapped by the impossibility of choice as Edgar is by his love?

A tempestuous household

The love of Catherine and Heathcliff is wild and tempestuous, she resorts to action, even physical violence, with great frequency, but this fits with Brontë's picture of life at Wuthering Heights. Note the remarkably casual way in which Nelly prepares for the return of Hindley by hiding the child and disabling his gun.

Chapter 9

In a drunken state, Hindley accidentally drops Hareton over the banisters and Heathcliff catches him. Catherine tells Nelly of her love for Edgar and Heathcliff. Nelly does not tell Catherine that Heathcliff has overheard their conversation. He leaves Wuthering Heights and Catherine falls ill. She goes to Thrushcross Grange to convalesce. Shortly afterwards, old Mr and Mrs Linton catch a fever and die. Catherine marries Edgar and becomes Mrs Linton.

Heathcliff saves Hareton

Hindley's drunkenness becomes worse and he turns violent, threatening Nelly and frightening Hareton. When Heathcliff saves Hareton from death, he instantly regrets it.

Catherine and love

Catherine tells Nelly that she has accepted Edgar's proposal of marriage. The

questions Nelly asks her show her down-to-earth attitude to life; Catherine's answers show her shallowness – she craves a better standard of living. Her dream about heaven reminds us of her ghost trying to get back into Wuthering Heights in Chapter 3. We also realise that her love for Heathcliff transcends life and death. It has no boundaries, moral or physical: they are soul-mates.

Love and passion

Heathcliff leaves, Catherine marries Edgar

Heathcliff hears Catherine say she would degrade herself by marrying him and

he leaves. Later, in Chapter 17, he throws a knife at Isabella because she refers to the 'degrading title of Mrs Heathcliff'. Note that, by leaving, Heathcliff misses Catherine's famous expression of their emotional and spiritual union: 'Nelly, I *am* Heathcliff'. In the same paragraph, beginning ' "It is not," retorted she', find some phrases from nature to describe the difference between her love for Edgar and for Heathcliff.

Nature

Love and marriage

This chapter contains the most striking commentary on Catherine's feelings on love and marriage: Nelly's catechism shows both why Catherine chooses Edgar and why it is a mistake. The 'It would degrade me to marry Heathcliff'/'I am Heathcliff' scene shows the impossibility of Catherine's situation.

When Heathcliff leaves there is a violent storm, and the fire in the hearth, always associated with Catherine, dies to an ember. It is as though Heathcliff's departure has unleashed the elements, and Catherine has killed her own 'fire'. Catherine becomes ill after her search for Heathcliff in the storm, and the illness is made worse by her guilt – she feels responsible for Heathcliff's disappearance, and is grief-stricken that he has gone. Her temper becomes more uncertain and she becomes mentally unstable. Three years after this, in April 1783, Catherine marries the infatuated Edgar, whose mother and father are now dead. Nelly goes with her to Thrushcross Grange, leaving little Hareton at Wuthering Heights.

Nelly is interrupted here: the date of the narration ends in April 1783, and we return to the present time. This is to preserve credibility and remind us that, extraordinary as these events are, they really happened in the past.

Chapter 10

In the 'present', Heathcliff visits Lockwood. Nelly resumes her narration: Heathcliff returns after three years' absence, and visits Catherine at Thrushcross Grange. Isabella Linton is attracted to him and falls in 'love'. Heathcliff moves back to Wuthering Heights where he assists in the systematic degradation of Hindley and his son Hareton.

Mr Lockwood continues the narrative, mentioning that Heathcliff called to see him. With this mention of Heathcliff, the reader realises that Lockwood knows only what he has witnessed at Wuthering Heights and what Nelly has told him up to Heathcliff's disappearance. Note that he views Nelly's narrative as little more than a romantic story (the 'hero' and 'heroine'): he hasn't comprehended the strength of Catherine and Heathcliff's relationship.

Heathcliff returns

To Nelly, Catherine and Edgar's marriage seems happy, apart from Catherine's

occasional moods of despair. When Heathcliff reappears, the description of him in shadow contrasts with the images of sunshine and light which have been used to describe Thrushcross Grange. When Nelly tells Edgar and Catherine of Heathcliff's arrival they are both looking out of the window over the moors and all is tranquil; but Heathcliff brings disruption. Catherine and Heathcliff talk as if Edgar isn't there: she is overexcited; he still talks of settling his score with Hindley.

After Heathcliff has left, Catherine tells Nelly of her joy. She is contemptuous of any feelings of envy which Edgar may have. To her, Edgar is incapable of passionate feeling and she knows her power over him: 'I believe I might kill him, and he wouldn't wish to retaliate.' This conversation echoes the one they had on the night of Heathcliff's disappearance.

Love and marriage

Catherine is 'breathless and wild, too excited to show gladness' at the return of Heathcliff. Her immediate reaction shows little regard for Edgar's feelings: 'Oh, Edgar darling, Heathcliff's come back!'. In one brief scene the foundation of the marriage is destroyed.

When Isabella falls in love with Heathcliff, Catherine points out his wolfish nature. Lockwood and Nelly have been deceived by him: Mr Lockwood sees Heathcliff as a loner like himself, while Nelly never realises quite how amoral Heathcliff is.

Heathcliff takes as much money in gambling as he can from Hindley. Joseph reports this to Nelly and his eye-witness account makes the situation credible. Note Brontë's facility in reproducing Northern dialect when Nelly recounts his speech to her.

Windows and eyes

Isabella is enraged by Heathcliff's and Catherine's contempt for her. Significantly, she too turns to violence when she feels they are in league against her. Heathcliff says that her eyes are like Edgar's. Remember his comments about their eyes in Chapter 6: 'the vacant blue eyes of the Lintons'. Heathcliff is interested in the fact that Isabella is Edgar's heir, but Catherine tells him to dismiss the idea of marrying her for her money. Nelly realises that Heathcliff's influence is becoming more powerful and she fears for the future, imagining him 'an evil beast', 'waiting his time to spring and destroy'.

Chapter 11

Nelly visits the Heights and witnesses how low its inhabitants have sunk. Heathcliff visits the Grange and begins to court Isabella. Catherine is informed of this and a dispute breaks out between Edgar and Heathcliff; Catherine intervenes. After Heathcliff has gone, she goes to her room and, locking herself in, becomes ill.

Nelly decides to warn Hindley of the danger he is in from Heathcliff. She meets Hareton at the gate, who curses and throws a stone at her but shows affection for Heathcliff, who is obviously seducing the child away from his father. Nelly runs away without talking to Hindley. She now fears

Heathcliff's evilness. (See Chapter 34 when she goes to see him in his room, thinks he looks like a goblin and drops her candle in fright.)

Heathcliff pursues Isabella

When Nelly realises Heathcliff is pursuing Isabella, she tells Catherine. Now Nelly becomes a participant in the drama: it is her intervention with Catherine and Edgar which precipitates the climax.

Catherine Earnshaw

Catherine confronts Heathcliff about Isabella. She is not jealous, but knows that his motives are not good and does not want him to be banned from visiting the Grange. She is disturbed by Heathcliff's lust for revenge and by his accusation that she has treated him 'infernally'.

Nelly tells Edgar about the scene she has just witnessed and she claims she wants to defend the peace of Thrushcross Grange: 'I fancied it could not be very prejudicial to Mrs Linton.' What follows shows just the opposite to be the case. One of the particular skills of Brontë's use of various narrators is the way in which Nelly Dean keeps her self-image (as a sensible helpful sort of person) even when her actions suggest otherwise. You can find other examples where she interferes to desperate effect whilst protesting her good sense.

Edgar confronts Heathcliff

Edgar resolves to banish Heathcliff from his house. However, Catherine locks
Imprisonment
out Edgar's men and Edgar is left to face Heathcliff alone. Catherine throws the key in the fire. This is another instance of imprisonment in the novel.

Though much of Heathcliff's behaviour is inexcusable, Edgar's lack of manhood is here presented with great contempt. It is not just Heathcliff and Catherine who sneer at him: 'Your type is not a lamb, it's a sucking leveret.' Read the paragraph beginning 'It did not need the medium of a flogging...' for a depiction of him as a pathetic creature, not to mention bringing in the gardeners and coachman.

Heathcliff and Catherine are united in their contempt for Edgar's cowardice. Edgar manages to escape and, before he returns with help, Heathcliff leaves. Edgar tries to make Catherine choose between him and Heathcliff, but she pleads illness. She throws a fit, which Nelly thinks is play-acting, but which awakens Edgar's concern. The next day, Edgar tells Isabella he will disown her if she sees Heathcliff again.

Chapter 12

Catherine is very ill, but Nelly keeps this from Edgar, who thinks the illness is self-induced. Meanwhile, Isabella elopes with Heathcliff.

Thrushcross Grange is in turmoil: Isabella weeps continuously, Catherine has shut herself in her room, and Edgar stays in the library. Nelly is convinced that she is the only sensible person at Thrushcross Grange.

Catherine is very ill, emotionally and physically

After three days, Catherine asks for food. She cannot understand why Edgar has not tried to see her but has buried himself in his books. Catherine's condition is much worse than Nelly realises: she sinks into a delirium, pulling the feathers from her pillow and remembering her childhood with Heathcliff. She imagines that she is back at Wuthering Heights and, seeing her reflection in the mirror, is convinced she sees a ghost. Feeling trapped, she implores Nelly to open the window so that she can breathe more air. It is a re-enactment of the scene from Chapter 3, except that there her ghost wants to be let in. We have been told these events not chronologically, but in accordance with the logic of the drama. The method of narration Brontë has chosen emphasises important events and creates dramatic tension.

Edgar is angry with Nelly for not informing him of Catherine's illness. Catherine is contemptuous of him and self-pitying by turns, predicting her own death. Finally, it is Nelly who fetches the doctor for Catherine.

Isabella elopes with Heathcliff

Nelly discovers about Isabella's elopement when she finds her bedroom empty. Earlier, she had found Isabella's dog being hanged, but had not realised the significance of it. The incident is typical of Heathcliff's savagery, which is not only physical but mental, hanging the dog which Isabella loves so much.

The elopement is narrated by Mary, one of the maids, giving the reader another eye-witness account. As Nelly becomes a character in the plot, her role as narrator becomes subsidiary. Edgar disowns Isabella when he learns she has eloped. He has an inflexible nature and is unable to tolerate anyone who flouts social convention.

Past, present and future

In Chapter 9, Catherine told Nelly: 'I have only to do with the present', to justify her marriage to Edgar. In Chapter 12, we see that her love for Heathcliff carries her beyond the present.

- She remembers her childhood at Wuthering Heights with Heathcliff.
- She prophesies her death, and burial in the open air.

Love and
passion

- She remembers her room, the fir outside the window, and prophesies that she will not rest until Heathcliff joins her in death — both of which look forward (for her) or back (for Lockwood and the reader) to the ghostly appearance in Chapter 3.

Examiner's tip

For the essay on page 63, and for many other essay titles on *Wuthering Heights*, you need to be aware of the novel's quality of simultaneously living in different times: by double narration, echoes of previous and future events and the imaginations of the characters.

■ Self-test questions Chapters 8–12

Uncover the plot

Delete two of the three alternatives given, to find the correct plot. Beware possible misconceptions and muddles.

Hareton/Hindley/Cathy is born: Frances recovers/dies/despairs: Hindley grows 'melancholy/desperate/religious'. Heathcliff has improved/left/deteriorated, but saves Cathy's/Hareton's/Nelly's life. Hearing Cathy say she hates/loves/pities Edgar, he leaves before she says she loves/hates/will marry him. Catherine/Heathcliff/Edgar catches fever. She marries Edgar/Heathcliff/Kenneth. The Lintons challenge/humour/constrain her, and they are happy. Heathcliff/Earnshaw/Hindley returns: Catherine is dismayed/excited/dismissive – and scornful because Nelly/Isabella/Edgar is upset. Heathcliff moves into the Grange/Heights/village, and gambles/fights/reconciles with Hindley. Isabella/Catherine/Mary is infatuated with Heathcliff, despite warnings from Edgar/Catherine/Nelly: Heathcliff is attentive/contemptuous/flattered, but attracted by her beauty/inheritance/kindness. Catherine and Nelly/Edgar/Heathcliff argue: Edgar finally confronts them, and Catherine falls ill. Kenneth prescribes quiet/fresh air/medicine – but Zillah/Nelly/Mary brings news that Heathcliff and Isabella have died/married/eloped.

Who? What? Why? How?

1 Who tells whom about (a) Isabella's infatuation, (b) Catherine and Heathcliff's argument over Isabella and (c) Isabella's elopement?
2 Whom does Heathcliff blame for his ill-treatment?
3 What is life like at the Heights after Frances' death?
4 What makes Catherine ill at first, and again later?
5 Why does Edgar not want Isabella to marry Heathcliff?
6 Why does Catherine 'adopt a double character' at Heights and Grange? When does it break down?
7 Why does Heathcliff leave Wuthering Heights – and why is this ironic?
8 How has Heathcliff deteriorated under Hindley's treatment ?
9 How does Catherine justify her decision to marry Edgar, and not Heathcliff?
10 How is Heathcliff 'transformed' when he returns from his absence, and what is the same?

Once upon a time...

1 What is the 'present time' now, and why are we made aware of it?
2 What periods of time does Nelly's story 'leap over' in these chapters?
3 What accounts by other people are included in Nelly's narrative?
4 What characteristics of Nelly's narration make us more cautious about adopting her point of view?
5 How does Catherine, ill, create a link with her own past and future, and with Lockwood's 'present'?

Familiar themes

1 Give TWO examples of imprisonment or locking in – one physical and one emotional.
2 Give THREE examples of Catherine's affinity for open air and the moors. Why is this ironic?
3 How is Heathcliff linked with the devil in his behaviour to (a) Hindley and (b) Catherine – and what mitigating factors are suggested?
4 Give TWO examples of an open window in these chapters. Note their symbolic significance.

What's love got to do with it?

1 About whom is the word 'infatuation' used, rather than 'love'? Why is this significant?
2 Why, according to Catherine, does she love Edgar?
3 Why, according to Catherine, does she love Heathcliff?
4 What images from nature does Catherine use to compare her love for Edgar and Heathcliff?
5 Give an example of a love/hate relationship, other than Heathcliff and Catherine.

Life cycle

List the events in these chapters linked to the cycle of birth, childhood, marriage, family, illness and death.

Chapter 13

Catherine eventually leaves her room and we discover that she is expecting a baby. Heathcliff and Isabella return to Wuthering Heights. Isabella takes up the narrative and, in a letter, describes her reception and life at the Heights.

Isabella writes to Nelly

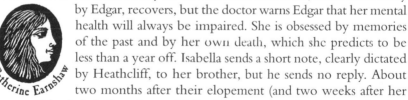

Heathcliff and Isabella are away for two months. Catherine, nursed devotedly by Edgar, recovers, but the doctor warns Edgar that her mental health will always be impaired. She is obsessed by memories of the past and by her own death, which she predicts to be less than a year off. Isabella sends a short note, clearly dictated by Heathcliff, to her brother, but he sends no reply. About two months after their elopement (and two weeks after her letter to Edgar), Isabella writes to Nelly. She recounts what happened to her when she returned to Wuthering Heights. She becomes the narrator for the rest of the chapter, giving a first-hand account of life at Wuthering Heights.

The last time Isabella was at Wuthering Heights was when Nelly was the housekeeper there. She compares the place as it is now with how it was then. Her distress heightens her powers of observation and this makes her account very vivid. She is incredulous and horrified at Heathcliff's behaviour: 'Is Mr Heathcliff a man? If so, is he mad? And if not, is he a devil?'

Joseph is unwelcoming and locks the gate behind them as 'if we lived in an ancient castle'. The exchanges between Joseph and Isabella are comic, as they highlight the differences in their upbringing and background. Isabella speaks to Hareton in an artificially affectionate way, but he rebuffs her with curses and threatens to set his dogs on her.

News of Hindley and Hareton

Isabella gets no more of a welcome from Hindley. He tells her that she must lock and bolt the door of Heathcliff's room, because he can't trust himself not to murder Heathcliff in revenge for impoverishing himself and Hareton. Heathcliff is evidently achieving his aim of degrading Hindley and his son.

Isabella angers Joseph by insisting on making the porridge because she sees him plunging his hands into the bowl of oatmeal, but her efforts are poor, much to his delight. When she asks Joseph to show her to her room he shows her a lumber room; and when asked for Heathcliff's room, he shows her Hindley's. Isabella hurls her dinner to the floor and breaks down: Joseph leaves her without a candle. Eventually she sleeps downstairs, only to be woken by Heathcliff who blames Edgar for Catherine's illness and says that Isabella will suffer for it, as she is Edgar's sister.

Isabella's letter is a vivid description of life at the Heights under Heathcliff's tyranny. It reiterates the intensity of Heathcliff's savage purpose and helps us to understand why Isabella later decides to leave the Heights.

Chapter 14

On learning of Isabella's return to the Heights, Edgar refuses to have anything to do with her, to the extent of refusing even to send her a note. Nelly goes to the Heights and, despite her better judgement, is persuaded by Heathcliff to take a letter from him to Catherine.

Nelly shows Edgar the letter from Isabella but he refuses to have any communication with her. Our sympathy is being turned away from Edgar in preparation for the dramatic events in Chapters 15 and 16. Nelly goes to Wuthering Heights and is disturbed by the deterioration of the house and by Isabella's lassitude. Nelly sees Heathcliff, who appears perfectly normal. She tells him that Catherine will always be an invalid, and he blames Edgar, saying that he would never have distressed her in the way Edgar has. This conversation reminds us of the one he had with Nelly in Chapter 7. Nelly tells Heathcliff that she hopes he will not try to see Catherine again; he gives an explanation of their love and emphasises its elemental quality.

Love and passion

The attack on Isabella

Heathcliff verbally attacks Isabella and his sadism is frightening. Nelly discovers

that he will not allow Isabella to leave the house and intends to keep her there until he provokes a response from Edgar. When Heathcliff thrusts Isabella from the room he tells Nelly: 'It is a moral teething; and I grind with greater energy, in proportion to the increase of pain'. He emphasises that he sees his plan of revenge as perfectly justified. His version of morality demands revenge for all he has suffered and he sees himself as an avenger against those who justly deserve punishment. (Note the parallel here with his later imprisonment of Cathy as a means of getting at Edgar.)

Heathcliff persuades Nelly to take a letter to Catherine, threatening to imprison her if she refuses. Again, this foreshadows events in Chapter 27 when he keeps Cathy and Nelly at Wuthering Heights. Nelly is unwilling to comply, but feels she has no option: 'I fear it was wrong, though expedient'.

Once again Nelly Dean's actions are questionable. Here she comes nearer than usual to admitting her guilt, but tries hard to justify what ultimately proves to be a fatal step: restoring communication between Catherine and Heathcliff. This is, after all, the faithful servant who, in the next chapter, can reflect, 'She's fainted or dead; so much the better.'

At the end of the chapter, Mr Lockwood returns briefly as narrator. In contrast to the passionate story Nelly relates, he talks shallowly about being careful in his future dealings with Catherine Heathcliff. This contrast highlights the strength of the passion between Heathcliff and Catherine.

Chapter 15

Nelly delivers Heathcliff's letter to Catherine, but she has no time to understand its contents before he arrives in person. He is upset by her sickly appearance. They cling to each other, despite Nelly's pleas that he should leave because Edgar is returning. Catherine will not let Heathcliff go, and collapses in his arms. When Edgar arrives, Heathcliff passes Catherine to him and leaves.

Heathcliff and Catherine reunited

When Edgar is in church, Nelly gives Heathcliff's letter to Catherine. It is four days since Nelly went to Wuthering Heights and Heathcliff has waited in the garden every night. In Chapter 34, Heathcliff takes four days to die, showing his powers of endurance.

Catherine is ill and her mind is enfeebled. Nelly imagines Catherine thinks about Wuthering Heights as she did when she was in her delirium in Chapter 13. Heathcliff enters the house and clasps Catherine in his arms. She accuses him of breaking her heart, and tortures him by asking how long he will remember her when she is dead. Nelly comments on Catherine's wild looks, her 'white cheek and bloodless lip' and is astonished at Heathcliff's display of emotion: 'he bestowed more kisses than ever he gave in his life before, I dare say'.

Love and marriage

The events just before and just after Catherine's death reveal only too clearly the power of Catherine and Heathcliff's love: a mutually destructive power. Both the descriptions and the dialogue in this chapter will provide you with much key material for this assignment.

This is the last time Catherine and Heathcliff meet while she is alive. The intensity of their love is indicated in both physical and emotional terms. Heathcliff grasps her arm so hard that he leaves four bruises on it where his fingers have been. They both talk of their love lasting beyond the grave, and of their torment while apart. Heathcliff accuses Catherine of betraying her own heart by marrying Linton, and breaking his own at the same time. Both seem to be aware of a different set of rules – outside conventional 'love' – which derive from their own passion for each other.

Love and passion

Catherine begs Heathcliff's forgiveness for doing 'wrong' by killing herself and making his life a misery too. Brontë seems to be saying that denying one's own feelings is wrong in terms of going against 'natural law' – the same as committing suicide. Catherine seems to be willing herself to death. Nelly, 'the cool spectator' is unmoved by Catherine's suffering – she considers it would be better for all concerned if Catherine were dead.

When Edgar comes in, Heathcliff thrusts the fainting Catherine into his arms and leaves, telling Nelly that he will be in the garden and that she should bring him news of Catherine's condition. Remember that she is seven months' pregnant at the time this interview takes place.

Chapter 16

At midnight, Cathy is born. Two hours later, Catherine dies. Nelly tells Heathcliff, who has been waiting in the garden. In his bitterness and despair he wishes Catherine to continue to be with him, even as a ghost. Allowed into the house by Nelly, he replaces Edgar's lock of hair with one of his own in Catherine's locket. Catherine is buried in the churchyard, near the moors.

A matter of inheritance

Note that Nelly mentions the legal issues which arise from Catherine giving birth to a girl. Unless Edgar has a son, Thrushcross Grange will pass to Isabella.

Catherine's death and Heathcliff's marriage to Isabella mean that Heathcliff will possess Thrushcross Grange when Edgar dies.

Catherine dies

In death, Catherine appears to have obtained the peace she so desired, but Edgar's expression bears only the 'hush of exhausted anguish'.

Given Lockwood's experiences in the opening chapters, do you think Catherine's spirit was at peace?

Catherine Earnshaw

When Heathcliff, waiting in the garden, is told of Catherine's death, he curses her and dashes his head against the tree trunk so that he draws blood. Nelly likens him to a savage beast, one of many instances where Heathcliff is described as an animal.

Heathcliff's exclamation that Catherine is not in heaven recalls her dream in Chapter 9, in which she was flung out of heaven, back to the middle of the heath at Wuthering Heights. Recall her words to Nelly then: 'I *am* Heathcliff', echoed by Heathcliff here: 'I *cannot* live without my life! I *cannot* live without my soul!'

Heathcliff

One night, Nelly leaves the window open and allows Heathcliff to say a last farewell to Catherine. After Heathcliff has gone, she notices he has taken Edgar's lock of hair from Catherine's locket and replaced it with his own. This

shows his determination to be with her in death. Remember he makes arrangements to have access to her coffin from his, when he is buried. Remember also how in Chapter 12, Catherine promised that when she was dead: 'I won't rest till you are with me... I never will!' Catherine is buried in the churchyard, very near to the open moor, as she prophesied in Chapter 12.

Nature

The new generation

Chapters 16 and 17 mark the end of the first half of the novel: in terms of both number of chapters and number of pages, they fall almost precisely at half-way. Of the first generation of main characters Catherine and Hindley die, Isabella leaves; of the next generation, Cathy and Linton are born. At the end of Chapter 17, more than a decade passes in a moment. What features and characters maintain the unity of the novel in these circumstances?

Chapter 17

Isabella escapes from Wuthering Heights and calls in at the Grange before leaving the area for ever. She takes up the narrative and describes a terrible fight between Heathcliff and Hindley. Nelly continues the narrative, mentioning that Isabella later had a son, Linton. We learn that Hindley died six months after Catherine and that his property, Hareton's birthright, has been mortgaged to Heathcliff.

Isabella flees Wuthering Heights

Isabella escapes from Wuthering Heights clad only in a light silk frock, despite the snowy weather. This emphasises her desperation to get away from Heathcliff. Her narration is full of violence and hatred. She describes Heathcliff's undisguised hatred for her and how her love for him has turned to hate: now she wishes he were dead. Note the vocabulary she uses – passionate hatred and horror make her language violent and emotional: 'Pulling out the nerves with red hot pincers, requires more coolness than knocking on the head.' Heathcliff is 'that incarnate goblin', 'monster' and 'the tyrant'. She has obviously changed from the starry-eyed girl who thought she had fallen in love with Heathcliff, and certainly she found the strength of will and determination, or desperation, to escape from the Heights.

Narration

This is a particularly striking example of Brontë's skill in using narrators. Isabella's hysterical account is extremely dramatic, but the incident also reveals Nelly Dean as the ideal listener. It is wiser not to speculate on the feats of memory that enable Lockwood to recall what Nelly told him of what Isabella told her of the exact words spoken by Heathcliff.

Isabella's description of Heathcliff's actions whilst he waited for news of Catherine shows his desperation, while Hindley's behaviour suggests he is near breaking-point. This prepares for the conflict she is shortly to describe.

She and Hindley continue to lock Heathcliff out of the house, but when Hindley announces his intention to kill Heathcliff, she says: 'treachery and violence are spears pointed at both ends', and warns Heathcliff of Hindley's intentions. She then confines her part to that of a passive observer, but **Imprisonment** cannot resist taunting Heathcliff about his love for Catherine.

Heathcliff struggles, unsuccessfully at first, to get in through the window – just as Catherine's ghost was unable to get in through the window of Lockwood's chamber. Finally, Heathcliff batters down the 'division between two windows' and throws himself at Earnshaw. With what Isabella calls 'preter-natural self-denial', he restrains himself from killing Hindley there and then.

Isabella's experience at the Heights has made her embrace Heathcliff's morality: 'his weakness was the only time when I could taste the delight of paying wrong for wrong.' Hindley survives this encounter, but the next day he and Heathcliff are fighting again. Isabella takes advantage of the confusion to escape. Notice the casual attitude towards violence at the Heights, and Isabella's new-found hardness in her throw-away remark: 'I knocked over Hareton, who was hanging a litter of puppies from a chairback'.

38

Isabella leaves Nelly, and we hear that she settles in London and gave birth to Linton, Heathcliff's son. Heathcliff does not try to make contact with her.

Edgar accepts Catherine's death with resignation, in contrast to Heathcliff. He grows to love his daughter Cathy.

Nelly hears of Hindley's death through Kenneth, the doctor, who tells her that Hindley drank himself to death, and was only twenty-seven years old when he died. Nelly has doubts about his, feeling that Heathcliff may have murdered him at last.

Chapter 18

Edgar goes south to visit Isabella. While he is away, Cathy explores beyond the grounds of Thrushcross Grange. She visits Wuthering Heights, meets Hareton, and discovers to her horror that he is her cousin.

Twelve years have passed and it is now 1797. The tragic emphasis of the novel is shown by the fact that these twelve years, 'the happiest of my life', receive such scant attention. The new generation of the Earnshaws and Lintons have grown up, and the next stage of Heathcliff's story now takes place.

Examiner's tip

In any essay dealing with the structure of the novel, Chapters 16–18 need close attention as the bridge between the two parallel narratives. Cathy is born, preparing for the next generation, Isabella disappears in two stages (London and death) and the method of **Narration** dispels twelve years in a moment.

Cathy's gentle prison

Cathy and her father spend a lot of time together, growing very close. She

Cathy

grows 'like a larch'. She is a beautiful child and her nature, although like her mother's in many ways, is not so fiery as Catherine's was. Consider whether Cathy embodies the best of the Earnshaws and the Lintons, the two families that produced her.

Imprisonment

Cathy is kept safe in the park at Thrushcross Grange but she is fascinated by what she can see of the world beyond it, and is curious to explore. She asks Nelly about Penistone Crags: Nelly answers in her commonsense way, but this doesn't stop Cathy making up 'fanciful tales'. There is no danger of her straying beyond the park: the gates are kept locked.

A new outsider arrives

At the beginning of the novel, Old Mr Earnshaw brought Heathcliff back with him from Liverpool. Now Edgar is to bring back Linton from London. Note the similarity here between the two arrivals: Linton, like Heathcliff, is a stranger to the area, an outsider. Just as Heathcliff was referred to as 'it', so he later refers to Linton, his own son, as 'it'.

While her father is away, Cathy escapes her 'prison', jumps the hedge of the park, and visits Wuthering Heights. She mistakes Hareton for a servant and he reacts angrily. She is horrified to learn he is her cousin, and lets out a piece of news which will no doubt be repeated to Heathcliff: Edgar has gone to London to bring Heathcliff's son back to Thrushcross Grange.

Nelly's description of Hareton helps to bring him more clearly into the narration at this point. Heathcliff has treated Hareton like a labourer and he lacks all formal education. However, Nelly recognises he has 'a mind owning better qualities than his father ever possessed'. His character is described in terms of nature: 'evidence of a wealthy soil that might yield luxuriant crops'. The fairy-tale element is strong here and it anticipates the relationship between the 'fairy princess' (Cathy) and her disguised 'prince' (Hareton).

Chapter 19

Isabella dies, and Edgar brings her son Linton home with him. On their arrival, Joseph comes with a demand from Heathcliff that Linton should be sent to the Heights immediately. Edgar refuses to disturb the child's sleep, but knows Linton will have to go early the next day.

Linton, Heathcliff's son

Cathy is delighted that her 'real' cousin is coming. Linton is described as a 'pale, delicate, effeminate boy' with a 'sickly peevishness in his aspect'. We are already prepared for his early death: only the robust can survive in that harsh Northern climate. Contrast him with Hareton: 'stout and healthy'. It is ironic that Heathcliff's son should resemble so closely the young Lintons as seen some years before through the windows of Thrushcross Grange. Cathy instantly takes to Linton, and makes 'a pet' of him, in contrast to her violent reaction against Hareton in the previous chapter.

Love and marriage

In the character of Linton Heathcliff, the dilemma of strength versus breeding reaches its peak. Linton never much progresses from the helpless child who 'can't sit on a chair' and is fed 'like a baby', but Cathy will later be charmed by his 'Linton' qualities in contrast to the rough-hewn Hareton.

Joseph arrives in his Sunday garments 'with his most sanctimonious and sourest face', to deliver Heathcliff's claim on his son. Joseph is, in part, a comic character, but the power of Heathcliff bodes ill for Linton.

Chapter 20

Linton is unwilling to go to his father, about whom Isabella has told him nothing. Nelly takes him and tries, unsuccessfully, to assure him that he will like his new life. At the Heights he is greeted by Heathcliff, who is dismayed at his son's sickly appearance.

Linton meets his father

Edgar's wish that Cathy should not be told of Linton's fate is unrealistic: it is inevitable that she will learn of Linton's whereabouts and that she will want to see him again.

Windows and eyes

Nelly calls Linton a 'poor thing' and evidently feels some sympathy for him: fast on his mother's death, the sickly lad travelled the long journey from London, stayed only one night at Thrushcross Grange, then was rudely awakened from his sleep and unceremoniously dumped at Wuthering Heights. On the ride there, Nelly tries to reassure him, but her reference to Heathcliff's 'black hair and eyes' prompts Linton's significant comment: 'Then I am not like him, am I?'

Linton's reception is anything but friendly. Heathcliff wonders if 'they reared it on snails, and sour milk', clearly disappointed by Linton's effeminate appearance. His comment: 'Damn my soul! But that's worse than I expected' suggests that he had some hopes for his son. He has also made arrangements for his education by engaging a tutor to visit three times a week. Nelly notes that it may be to Linton's advantage that his father needs to preserve Linton's life in order to bring about his full revenge on Edgar. References to Linton being 'property' and Heathcliff's words 'he's mine' swiftly reassert the reality of Heathcliff's views about and plans for Linton.

Another prisoner

Imprisonment

As Nelly leaves, Linton calls out to her, but he is locked in: 'The latch was raised and fell – they did not suffer him to come forth'. Heathcliff now has two of the next generation in his power. Linton is certainly not free, but we may wonder how restricted Hareton is. He does not strike one as being easily confined – any more than Heathcliff was by Hindley some years before.

■ Self-test questions Chapters 13–20

Uncover the plot
Delete two of the three alternatives given, to find the correct plot. Beware possible misconceptions and muddles.

Isabella tells Nelly/Edgar/Catherine about her arrival at the Grange/Heights/village: only the servant/child/dog was kind. Heathcliff shows affection/cruelty/indifference to Isabella and forces Nelly/Joseph/Edgar to let him see Catherine. Violently hitting/holding/cursing each other – tormented by thoughts of her death/marriage/pregnancy – they forgive/forget/hate each other. Catherine dies/recovers/revives after Cathy/Linton/Hareton is born. Heathcliff cries: 'I cannot live without my love/revenge/soul!' Isabella plots with Hindley/Hareton/Joseph against him, and flees to Gimmerton/Thrushcross/London. Hindley/Edgar/Heathcliff dies soon after: Nelly is relieved/indifferent/ grieved; Heathcliff is master of the Grange/Heights/district. Edgar fetches Hareton/Cathy/Linton from a dying Isabella. Cathy discovers the Heights/Crags/village, meets Linton/Hareton/Heathcliff, and won't accept he is her brother/servant/cousin. She makes a 'friend/pet/enemy' of Linton, but he is claimed by Edgar/Nelly/Heathcliff, who plans to make him a servant/gentleman/brute, as an instrument of reconciliation/redemption/revenge.

Who? What? Where? Why? How?
1 Who is accused of breaking whose heart, in the last meeting of Catherine and Heathcliff?
2 Who/what are the instruments of Heathcliff's revenge on (a) Edgar and (b) Hindley in these chapters?
3 What 'double cause' does Edgar have to desire Catherine's recovery – and why is this ominous?
4 What bodes ill for Linton's life at the Heights and what bodes well?
5 Where is Catherine buried, and why is this significant?
6 Why does Heathcliff say he wants revenge on Edgar – and what other views of this are there?
7 Why does Hindley fight his urge to kill Heathcliff, and refuse to banish him from the Heights?
8 How does Cathy react to Hareton and to Linton? Why does this become significant?
9 How do (a) Heathcliff and (b) Edgar take Catherine's death?
10 How does Isabella drive Heathcliff to violence – and why?

Once upon a time…
1 Who narrates events at Wuthering Heights after Heathcliff's 'honeymoon' – and to what effect?
2 Give TWO examples where the 'present' breaks into the narrative, and note the effect created.
3 Where is there a 12-year 'leap' in the narrative – and what does this accomplish?

Familiar themes
1 Give TWO examples of (a) locking out and (b) locking in, in these chapters. Where are they set?
2 Give an example of the mixture of hate and love Isabella has for Heathcliff.
3 List phrases from Heathcliff and Catherine's last meeting which show the violence of their passion.

4   What natural images does Heathcliff use to show the inadequacy of Edgar's love? What does this echo?

Till death do us part?
1   How does Catherine taunt Heathcliff with the thought of her death?
2   How does Catherine imagine their love lasting beyond death?
3   We saw Catherine's ghost (3) and heard her say 'I won't rest till you are with me' (9). What echo do we hear in these chapters?
4   What symbolic tokens are used to unite Heathcliff, Cathy and Edgar in death?
5   How does Edgar love Catherine beyond death?

Chapter 21

Another three years pass. On Cathy's sixteenth birthday she is given permission to go to the moors with Nelly. They meet Heathcliff and Hareton and are persuaded to visit the Heights, where Cathy again meets Linton. Heathcliff confides to Nelly that he wants Linton and Cathy to marry. During the visit, Cathy hears Heathcliff's side of the conflict between himself and Edgar. On her return home, Edgar gives his view of the dispute. Cathy begins a secret correspondence with Linton, but Nelly discovers it.

Nelly's report of her conversation with the housekeeper at Wuthering Heights describes how Linton is surviving there. Nelly's conclusion that Linton had become 'selfish and disagreeable' prepares us for his actions later when he helps Heathcliff to deceive Cathy. Note that Nelly feels guilty about leaving Linton at Heathcliff's mercy. The advantage of the flashback method of narration is again evident here: we can skip three years to the next significant event in the story: Cathy's visit to the moors when she is sixteen.

Marriage plans

Nelly notes of Cathy that it was 'a pity she could not be content'. This is seen

Cathy

in the way Cathy outstrips Nelly and strays too far on the moor, so that she chances upon Heathcliff and Hareton. She is easily persuaded to visit the Heights again, despite Nelly's opposition. Heathcliff unveils his plans for Cathy and Linton to Nelly, displaying accurate knowledge of the inheritance laws of the time. Given his determination for revenge, this is not surprising.

Heathcliff

Heathcliff explains to Cathy why he and Edgar hate each other. He claims that it was because of Edgar's snobbery that they quarrelled: Edgar did not think Heathcliff good enough to marry Isabella. This simplification of events omits his relationship with Catherine and puts Edgar in the wrong in his daughter's eyes.

The attraction that Catherine found in Edgar finds its parallel in Cathy and Linton: she thinks he is a 'gentleman'.

Heathcliff's comments about Hareton: 'twenty times a day I covet Hareton with all his degradation... I'd have loved the lad if he had been some one else' show that Heathcliff works hard to suppress his human affections, turning his appreciation of Hareton's good qualities into enjoyment at his degradation.

Cathy and Linton

Hareton Earnshaw

Cathy and Linton make fun of Hareton's inability to read, a reminder of those times when Heathcliff was mocked by Edgar for his lack of refinement. Heathcliff 'cast a look of singular aversion on the flippant pair': his sympathies, almost despite himself, lie with Hareton in this situation. Do you think Heathcliff shows signs of mellowing here?

Examiner's tip

To explain the effect of the 'two halves' of the novel, you need good evidence of the mirroring of events in each half. Linton mocking Hareton as 'a colossal dunce', Hareton threatening to 'fell thee this minute' recall Edgar sneering at Heathcliff's unkempt appearance and receiving a tureen of apple sauce for his pains.

Cathy

Edgar tells Cathy the real reasons for the hatred between Heathcliff and himself but, despite her father's warnings, Cathy still wants to see Linton. As a substitute for visiting, she begins a secret correspondence. When Nelly finds the letters from Linton, she suspects Heathcliff has had a hand in writing them in order to encourage the relationship.

Chapter 22

Edgar falls ill, and Nelly accompanies Cathy on her walks. One day they meet Heathcliff, who tells Cathy that Linton is unwell and missing her desperately. Cathy, on the understanding that Heathcliff will be away, resolves to visit Linton the next day.

Nature

The story passes rapidly from March to November. We are now approaching 1801, the year of the 'present day' narration in the novel (see Chapter 1). Nelly's description contrasts the young, carefree Cathy with the new, sadder one. The weather, cold and damp, reflects Cathy's lack of spirits and Edgar's ill-health. Cathy has a premonition about Edgar's death, which Nelly does her best to calm. Cathy gets locked the wrong side of a wall which borders the road and it is here that Heathcliff chances upon her – when she and Nelly are in a position of powerlessness.

Heathcliff plays on Cathy's conscience

Heathcliff takes his chance to play on Cathy's affection for her cousin and her sense of guilt. He bullies her into believing that she is to blame for her cousin's unhappiness and dramatises Linton's illness, saying that he might easily die. Coming at a time when she is depressed, the news of Linton's ill health worries Cathy still more, and she persuades Nelly to let her visit Linton.

Chapter 23

Cathy and Nelly visit Linton, who is not well. He and Cathy quarrel and he seems to become worse. On their way home, Nelly tells Cathy that she must not visit again. However, Nelly falls ill and is confined to bed. During this time, Cathy secretly visits Linton at the Heights.

Linton is persuaded he would like to marry Cathy

We learn much about Linton in this section of the novel. His ideas on love

Heathcliff

are clearly influenced by Heathcliff: 'papa says you would love me better than him, and all the world, if you were my wife'. Heathcliff has already told Nelly that he wants Cathy and Linton married to make sure of his power over the Earnshaw and Linton households, and he has persuaded Linton that his salvation from the brutal regime at Wuthering Heights lies in marrying Cathy.

Linton uses his illness to blackmail affection from Cathy. He convinces her that she has both hurt and upset him and she gets into such a state that she responds to his wheedling cries and pretended distress.

Place
Between the Grange and the Heights is open moorland, where characters can be free and/or in personal danger. Both the houses offer security, but also imprisonment: there are many instances where both become literally or metaphorically prisons.

Returning to Thrushcross Grange, Cathy says to Nelly: ' "The Grange is not a prison, Ellen, and you are not my jailer." ' Her words, though brave, should make us uneasy, especially when Nelly makes the ironic comment: ' "I'm glad you have no chance of having him for a husband" '. Nelly is perhaps being wilfully short-sighted here, given Heathcliff's stated intentions of seeing them married, Edgar's poor health, and Cathy's impressionable nature. Her prediction that Linton will not 'win twenty' will prove to be accurate.

Chapter 24

When she recovers, Nelly discovers that Cathy has been visiting Linton. Cathy recounts her secret visits to Nelly, tells her what she feels and makes an effective narrator. The chapter has echoes of the past and pointers to the future.

Ideas of 'heaven'

Nature

Linton and Cathy discuss their ideas of heaven and their ideas are completely opposed. Linton looks for the quiet and still of a summer's day but Cathy's desire is for life, motion and vigour: ' "I said his heaven would be only half alive, and he said mine would be drunk; I said I should fall asleep in his, and he said he would not breathe in mine…" '

Learning to read

The first indication that Cathy is beginning to have an effect on Hareton is

Hareton Earnshaw

seen when he shows her that he has learnt to read the inscription above the door: significantly, it is his own birthright that he learns to read first. However, rebuffed by Cathy because he cannot read the numbers, he turns on Linton. You can see here a parallel with Heathcliff who, thinking he was rejected by Catherine, turned on Edgar. Note also Hareton's treatment of books here: he kicks one to the side, symbolically rejecting Cathy.

Cathy is horrified at Hareton's savagery and at Linton's response: 'If you don't let me in I'll kill you!' This echoes the fight between Hindley and Heathcliff as reported by Isabella in Chapter 17.

Irritated by Linton's moodiness, Cathy decides to end the relationship,

Love and passion

which provokes Linton to confide in her. He appears to be caught up in a web of self-disgust and misery which makes him cruel, spiteful and self-pitying. This scene and the one in which Hareton locks Cathy and Linton out of the room are charged with greater feeling than anything since Chapter 17 and signifies a quickening of the story's pace. Cathy pities Linton and mistakes her pity for love.

When Hareton tries to make amends to Cathy, she uses her whip on him as she rides away. Again the environment of Wuthering Heights seems to bring out the cruellest, most violent aspects of people's characters.

Nelly is furious at what she has learned and tells Edgar, who bans further visits to the Heights.

Chapter 25

Linton has been allowed to write to Edgar, who is very ill. Linton's letters stress his affection for Cathy. Edgar, worrying what will happen to Cathy when he dies, eventually agrees that the two shall be allowed to meet on the moors. It is Nelly's belief that Heathcliff has a hand in composing the letters, in view of his wish that the two should marry and the fact that Linton is now very ill.

The timing of the action is mentioned and events now begin to move more rapidly. Nelly's narrative has now reached February 1801.

Edgar considers Cathy's future

Edgar knows he is dying and, whilst happy at the thought of joining Catherine in death, is distressed that Cathy will be alone – he is not sure about Linton as a prospective husband and knows he is 'only a feeble tool to his father'.

Linton pleads with Edgar by letter to allow Cathy and him meet on the moors, but nobody outside the Heights knows how ill he is. The last paragraph of this chapter mentions the extent of Heathcliff's determination to pursue his revenge. Nelly later learns that Heathcliff bullied and threatened Linton into taking walks on the moors, even though he was dying.

Chapter 26

Cathy and Linton meet, but nearer to the Heights than Nelly had expected. Cathy and Nelly are shocked by Linton's poor state of health and by his fear of Heathcliff. They promise to meet again the following week.

Summer is now over and Cathy goes to see her cousin. It is clearly Heathcliff's doing to tempt them nearer to Wuthering Heights than they expected, as though Linton is bait to attract the intended victim. The moors, to where Catherine and Heathcliff escaped for peace and freedom when they were young, are now used by Heathcliff as the setting for Cathy's abduction. Cathy finds

Nature Linton's attitude and manner distasteful, her previous affection for her cousin being quite forgotten. The 'interview', as Cathy calls it, is plainly undertaken by Linton only because Heathcliff commands it, and Linton is terrified of the consequences if he does not comply, pleading with Cathy not to look unhappy if Heathcliff sees her.

Chapter 27

Edgar is now seriously ill and Cathy is reluctant to leave him, but she fulfils her promise to see Linton again. Linton is desperately ill. Heathcliff arrives and persuades them to help Linton back to the Heights, but once there they are locked in. Linton confesses he knows of Heathcliff's intentions – that he and Cathy should marry. Cathy makes a spirited attack on Heathcliff but is subdued by blows from him. She and Nelly are locked up for the night. In the morning, Cathy and Linton are to be married.

Linton's terror

It is a week later, and Cathy has to see Linton again. She tries to rouse some courage in him, for he is obviously in a state of abject terror of Heathcliff. Linton is desperate that Cathy should not leave, but she has lost patience with his cowardice. Linton's words: 'You *will* consent – and he'll let me die with you' perhaps describes the gravity of Heathcliff's threat to Linton.

Prisoners

Heathcliff locks the door as soon as Cathy and Nelly are in the house, turning the Heights into their prison. Note the intensity of Heathcliff's hatred: 'Had I been born where laws are less strict, and tastes less dainty, I should treat myself to a slow vivisection of those two, as an evening's amusement… By hell! I hate them.' Cathy attempts to regain the key, an event which echoes

Imprisonment Catherine's taking the key from Edgar and Isabella's refusal to open the door to Heathcliff earlier in the novel. Cathy suffers dearly for the attempt: Heathcliff's brutal attacks on her and on Nelly are more violent than anything Cathy has ever encountered before.

Having followed his father's instructions, Linton recovers some strength and we see him at his worst: he is totally self-centred, pitiful and cowardly.

Heathcliff makes clear his intentions for Cathy. She will agree to the marriage if Heathcliff will allow her to see her father Edgar before he dies. The fact that Edgar's grief will be compounded by Cathy's absence gives Heathcliff pleasure. Nelly is locked up alone and kept prisoner for five nights.

Narration

The advantages of Brontë's complex system of narration are many. Here mystery builds up while the main narrator is taken out of the action. There is no omniscient narrator, so the reader shares Nelly's anxiety and ignorance of events outside her prison.

Chapter 28

When Nelly is released, she learns that Cathy and Linton are married. She goes to Thrushcross Grange where she discovers Edgar close to death. Cathy arrives, having escaped from Wuthering Heights. Edgar dies in her arms.

Linton and Cathy are married

Heathcliff

Nelly is released by Zillah. She discovers that Heathcliff has made up a story to explain her and Cathy's disappearance. She is horrified by the unfeeling way in which Linton describes the last few days of Cathy's treatment.

The brutal treatment of Cathy by Heathcliff, especially when he grinds Edgar's portrait into the ground and hits her, cutting open her lip, shows that the success of his plans has not sated his thirst for revenge.

Cathy escapes, Edgar dies

Cathy escapes by climbing out of the very window by which Catherine's ghost tried to enter in Chapter 3, and she uses the fir tree which woke Lockwood

 to help her reach the ground. Edgar has tried to arrange to change his will, but Heathcliff's plans have been well laid. The lawyer does not come before Edgar has died in Cathy's arms. When the lawyer does arrive, we learn that 'He had sold himself to Mr Heathcliff', and he carries out Heathcliff's instructions to close Thrushcross Grange.

Windows and eyes

■ Self-test questions Chapters 21–28

Uncover the plot

Delete two of the three alternatives given, to find the correct plot. Beware possible misconceptions and muddles.

Cathy and Edgar/Nelly/Linton, meeting Heathcliff/Linton/Joseph on the moor, visit the Kirk/Grange/Heights. Linton, weak but athletic/graceful/spirited, joins Cathy in mocking Nelly/Heathcliff/Hareton. Edgar warns that Heathcliff is a 'charming/harsh/diabolical man', but Cathy/Nelly/Edgar exchanges letters/tokens/books with Linton: Nelly/Edgar/Heathcliff burns them. Heathcliff/Hareton/Linton tells her Linton is dying of a fever/broken heart/cold: Cathy secretly visits/forgets/leaves him when Heathcliff/Nelly/Edgar is ill. They fight with Heathcliff/Hareton/Joseph, argue – then part/reconcile/marry. Nelly tells Heathcliff/Hareton/Edgar: Cathy is forbidden/allowed/told to visit again. Linton writes to Cathy/Nelly/Edgar, asking to see Cathy. They meet near the Grange/Heights/village – Linton is apathetic/amorous/asleep – and again, when Edgar is better/dying/dead: Cathy is loving/sympathetic/impatient, Linton terrified/indignant/languid. Taking him home, Cathy and Nelly/Linton/Hareton are entertained/imprisoned/ejected by Heathcliff, who forces Cathy to marry/nurse/amuse Linton. Nelly, freed by Hareton/Zillah/Linton, runs to Edgar/Green/Kenneth. Cathy escapes: her father/brother/cousin dies.

Who? What? Where? Why? How?

1   Who is the only person Heathcliff does not appear to hate at this period, and why?
2   What traits do we see in Linton (a) when Cathy visits him at the Heights, and (b) after their marriage?
3   What does Heathcliff force Linton to do, in order to trap Cathy? Why does Linton comply?
4   What reason does Heathcliff give Cathy for Edgar's 'prejudice' against him, and why?
5   What good qualities are we told about in Hareton: how does Heathcliff view this?

6   Where does Cathy (a) run into Heathcliff and (b) arrange to meet Linton?
7   Why does Heathcliff want Linton to marry Cathy?
8   How does Heathcliff trick Cathy into visiting Linton? How does he finally force her to marry him?
9   How do Cathy's feelings for Linton change?
10   How does Edgar finally try to thwart Heathcliff's plans, and how is he prevented from doing so?

Once upon a time...
1   At what points is Nelly 'removed' from the action, and who fills the gap as narrator?
2   What date is given for the action in Chapter 21, 22, 25 and 27, and why is this significant?
3   How is Lockwood's role as narrator re-established in these chapters and why?

Familiar themes
1   Which characters are ill in these chapters, and with what effect on the plot?
2   Give THREE examples of the use of books in these chapters, plus a significant piece of literacy, or reading.
3   What are Cathy's and Linton's ideas of 'heaven' in nature?
4   What season is described (a) before Cathy meets Heathcliff for the first time and (b) when Edgar falls ill?
5   What kind of 'love' does Cathy have for Linton, and what reminders do we get of a greater passion?
6   How does Edgar approach death? Where does this find an echo in the novel?

Parallel lines
What 'echoes' do we get of the following events from earlier chapters (identified in brackets)?
1   Catherine, liking Edgar's fair looks and 'gentlemanly' qualities, accuses Heathcliff of being boorish (8)
2   Isabella and Hindley lock out Heathcliff, who threatens them if they do not let him in (17)
3   Nelly tells Edgar Heathcliff is with Cathy (11). Rebuked, she doesn't tell him about his final visit (12)
4   Catherine, at the Grange, longs to be in her room at the Heights, with 'the firs by the lattice' (12)

Chapter 29

After Edgar's funeral, Heathcliff takes possession of his property and Cathy has to return to Wuthering Heights. Heathcliff describes to Nelly how, when Edgar's grave was being prepared, he persuaded the grave diggers to alter Catherine's coffin so that he will be able to 'reach through' when he is buried next to her. Cathy returns to the Heights with Heathcliff.

Heathcliff avenged

Nelly and Cathy wait in the library at Thrushcross Grange for Heathcliff to arrive to claim his property. Nelly looks around the room and remembers the time, eighteen years before, when Heathcliff returned after three years' absence on a similar autumn night in the darkness, and began the conflict that was to end in Catherine's death.

Heathcliff tells Cathy that he has punished Linton for aiding her in her escape and that Linton hates her because he has suffered. Cathy tells Heathcliff that nobody loves him and that he is as lonely as the devil. Her words cause Heathcliff to order her from the room.

Heathcliff recounts his visit to Catherine's grave. This is the second time

 he becomes a narrator and shows his own feelings, without another person's views diluting or analysing them. Heathcliff tells Nelly how he uncovered Catherine in her coffin and her face was still preserved. Remember Mr Lockwood's description of Gimmerton Kirk in his dream in Chapter 3:

Love and passion 'whose peaty moisture is said to answer all the purposes of embalming', almost as though nature preserves her for Heathcliff. He tells Nelly that the previous night he dreamt he was 'sleeping' – in death – next to Catherine, and that since then he has felt peace at last.

Love and marriage

Heathcliff and Catherine's relationship lies outside the area of choice. Though he speaks of 'her darling head', most of his speech tells of agony and the need to find relief and be 'pacified': 'she showed herself, as she often was in life, a devil to me!'.

Another view of events at Wuthering Heights

He tells how, on the day of her funeral, he returned to her grave to get her body out of the coffin. As he was dismantling the coffin he felt a warm breath and knew her spirit was near. Heathcliff rushed back to Wuthering Heights, talking to her, sure of her presence, but when he arrived he found Isabella and Hindley had locked him out (Chapter 17). This was why he was so furious

 and desperate to enter – and so tormented and grief-stricken the following day: Catherine would not show herself. Ever since, he says, he has been 'the sport of that intolerable torture': remember that he challenged Catherine to do this, on hearing of her death ('Drive me mad! Only do not leave

Imprisonment me!') in Chapter 16. Heathcliff is trapped at Wuthering Heights, waiting for Catherine to appear to him. He feels 'pacified... a little' by having seen her in the grave. Yet not long after this conversation, Lockwood's visit (Chapter 3) brings the frustration back: Catherine has visited, and Heathcliff still has not seen her. This is an example of how Brontë uses the time-scheme of the novel to highlight important events and interpret the past in the light of the present.

Chapter 30

Zillah takes the narrative. She describes how Cathy tried to nurse Linton, but that he died shortly after. Cathy remains in her room for a while. When she eventually leaves it, she rebuffs Hareton's attempts to be friendly.

Linton dies

Cathy

Zillah is the housekeeper at Wuthering Heights. She is a mean-minded woman and tells of Cathy's suffering from her own, unfeeling viewpoint. Zillah tells Nelly this about a month before Mr Lockwood's first visit. Cathy is left to nurse Linton on her own and Heathcliff refuses to send for a doctor. When Linton dies, Cathy says she feels like death. She is now destitute, because all her property falls to Heathcliff, who forced Linton to write a will when Cathy escaped to Thrushcross Grange. She remains in her room for a fortnight after Linton's death. Remember that Catherine locked herself in her room in Thrushcross Grange in Chapter 12.

Books

Hareton tries to improve his appearance, with Zillah's help, to make himself more presentable for Cathy. This is a reminder of Nelly helping Heathcliff to look more presentable for the Linton's visit in Chapter 7. Cathy makes for the fire and we are reminded of Chapter 2 when Lockwood discovers her by the hearth. Notice her attitude towards books. To Catherine books were objects, to Cathy they offer escape. Cathy is very much like her father. Hareton sees books as a means of self-improvement, and Zillah asks Cathy to read aloud from them, but she haughtily refuses.

Mr Lockwood takes up the narration again. He is going to see Heathcliff to tell him he is going back to London. It is January 1802. The narrative has come full circle and we are back in the 'present day', with Lockwood as narrator.

Chapter 31

Lockwood goes to Wuthering Heights and takes a note for Cathy from Nelly. It is intercepted by Hareton, and it is seen that he and Cathy are still on bad terms.

Books

This time Lockwood visits the Heights, he notices the gate is still locked, but now he knows the reason. Hareton unlocks the gate and follows him in, and when Lockwood gives Cathy the letter from Nelly, Hareton snatches it first. However, he relents when Cathy cries: he is evidently fond of her and has a tender heart, despite his harsh upbringing. Cathy says she has no books as Heathcliff has destroyed most of them and Hareton stole the rest. She ridicules Hareton's attempts to read and Lockwood defends his attempts at self-improvement, displaying sensitivity towards Hareton's embarrassment.

Heathcliff prepares for death

Heathcliff

When Heathcliff arrives, Lockwood notices a difference: he appears anxious, preoccupied and thinner than when we last saw him. From what he said to Nelly, we know that he has begun to brood on his own death; he is obsessed by the thought of being reunited with Catherine. Lockwood tells him that he is leaving Thrushcross Grange and Heathcliff assures him that he expects to be paid the full rent. Again, Lockwood's insensitivity is apparent when he imagines forming a relationship with Cathy as being 'more romantic than a fairy tale'. He can't appreciate that the transformation of Hareton from a 'clown' to a civilised man will be more of a 'fairy tale'. His words betray the fact that he has withdrawn from the real world of emotion, as Linton and Isabella did, and sees life only in terms of a literary convention.

Narration

At the end of Chapter 30, 'thus ended Mrs Dean's story.' Now Lockwood bids Heathcliff adieu and rides away. The story seems to be over, framed by Lockwood's visits to the Heights and his grotesque misunderstandings. But Chapter 32 will start like Chapter 1, for something that is more than an Epilogue.

Chapter 32

Some months later, Lockwood finds himself in the neighbourhood again, and, on impulse, visits Wuthering Heights. He discovers that Hareton and Cathy are reconciled and that their relationship is developing into love. Shortly after Lockwood left for London, Zillah left the Heights and Nelly moved in as housekeeper. She tells him of events up to Heathcliff's death, which occurred three months previously.

New life at Wuthering Heights

Nature

Mr Lockwood returns to Yorkshire for the shooting season in September 1802. He sees the harvest coming in from Gimmerton and this reminds him of Thrushcross Grange. He walks over the moors, commenting on their beauty in summer and savagery in winter; he also notices Gimmerton Kirk. These are all symbolic references to the lives of Catherine, Edgar and Heathcliff.

Arranging for the housekeeper at Thrushcross Grange to prepare the house for the night, he goes to Wuthering Heights, having heard that Nelly is now

Imprisonment

housekeeper there. When he arrives, the gates, doors and windows are all open, flowers bloom, and he can see a glowing fire through the window. Hareton and Cathy are framed in the open window, reading. No longer a prison, the atmosphere of the Heights is warm and welcoming. Contrast Lockwood's first visit in Chapter 1. Joseph strikes the only sour note: he sees Hareton's happiness as a sign he is bewitched! When Lockwood approaches Nelly Dean, she is 'sewing and singing a song'.

Love and
passion

Nelly tells Lockwood that Heathcliff died the previous May. She takes up the narration for the last time and tells of the growing love between Hareton and Cathy and how Cathy has begun to civilise him through education and books. Nelly tells Mr Lockwood that when Hareton and Cathy marry she will be the happiest woman in England. Their happy love contrasts to all the other kinds of love in the book.

Chapter 33

There is a confrontation between Heathcliff and Cathy, but he seems to lack the energy to pursue the dispute. He tells Nelly that he has lost all desire for revenge, even though he has the remaining members of the Linton and Earnshaw families within his power.

Cathy and Hareton decide to rearrange the garden and replace some of Joseph's currant bushes with plants from Thrushcross Grange. This symbolically reflects the union of the Grange and the Heights which comes about with the marriage of Hareton and Cathy. Hareton's laughter infuriates Heathcliff, and Cathy's defiant accusation that he has robbed both her and Hareton of their inheritances provokes Heathcliff to attack her. But he finds he is powerless, partly because Cathy reminds him of her mother ('those infernal eyes') and partly because he senses Catherine's spirit is near. Note that although Hareton does not wish Cathy to be hurt, he will not side with her against Heathcliff: he bears Heathcliff no ill-will for the way he has been treated and feels loyalty towards him. Hareton exhibits true Christian forgiveness here: note that Cathy earlier forgave Heathcliff (Chapter 27), and spares him from now on.

The destruction of his garden convinces Joseph that Cathy is a witch.

Heathcliff tells Nelly what he is feeling, the third time he has done so in the novel (see Chapters 6 and 29 for the others). He admits he has lost his taste for revenge and he sees the irony of this. It is not that he has discovered a streak of humanity, simply that he is 'too idle to destroy for nothing'. He now has within his power two people who are a continual reminder of his loss, and consequently a torture to him. We begin to comprehend the torment he has been living through since Catherine's death. He yearns for death to release him. Nelly reminds Lockwood that this was the Heathcliff he first met.

Chapter 34

Heathcliff is full of nervous energy, eating little, and excited, as though expecting something to happen. He locks himself in the room where Lockwood had his dream and is found there the next morning, dead. The window is open. Cathy and Hareton are to be married in the new year, to Nelly's delight.

It is April. Cathy and Hareton continue their relationship, and the weather is mild. Heathcliff's behaviour has become more erratic: he has been out all night

Love and passion

and when he comes back appears to be strangely excited. Remember how agitated he became when he heard that Lockwood had seen Catherine's ghost in Chapter 3. He tells Nelly that he is in sight of heaven, meaning that Catherine's spirit is near. There are several versions of 'heaven' in the novel: Catherine's in Chapter 9; Linton's and Cathy's in Chapter 24. Heathcliff retires to a darkened room, listening

to the brook at Gimmerton – a reminder of how Catherine sat with a 'vague, distant look' at Thrushcross Grange in Chapter 15, just before her last illness and death.

Heathcliff begins his vigil for Catherine

That night, Heathcliff sleeps in the panelled bed, hoping that Catherine will come to him there. On the second day he appears to be watching something which is invisible to everyone else. He rejects food, and that night Nelly hears him talking aloud, muttering Catherine's name. On the third day, Nelly reminds him of the Christian view of heaven: he replies that he has nearly

Heathcliff

attained his heaven. Consider what the novel has to say about conventional religion – the only devoutly religious character in the book is Joseph, who is presented frequently comically, as lacking Christian virtues. Heathcliff tells Nelly to make sure that his arrangements for the coffins are carried out. Remember that in Chapter 29 he told Nelly he had arranged

with the sexton to have the side of Catherine's coffin lowered so that in death they could be together. On the fourth day he stays in his room, and next morning Nelly finds him dead, the bedroom window open, and his bedclothes drenched with rain. The final horror is his expression: his eyes are wide open and will not close and his lips are parted in a sneer of contempt.

Reunited

Heathcliff's expression of exultation perhaps shows that he has been reunited with Catherine in death, but Nelly is frightened lest anyone else should see it. Compare Catherine's expression in death: an 'untroubled image of Divine rest' (Chapter 16). After Heathcliff's death, there are rumours that he and Catherine haunt the moors. A little boy tells Nelly that he has seen them and that they frightened him. It is fitting that Catherine and Heathcliff are destined to haunt the moors whose wildness reflected the tempestuous nature of their love.

Nature

Examiner's tip

The way the novel ends, aided by the unusual **Narration**, unites both halves: two pairs of lovers share the last page, one united only in death, the other a lighter, more controlled version of the first pair and 'afraid of nothing'.

Nelly tells Lockwood that Hareton and Cathy are to be married in the new year, uniting the Linton and Earnshaw families, and will live at Thrushcross Grange. Catching sight of Hareton and Cathy, Lockwood observes with unconscious irony: 'Together they would brave Satan and all his legions.' Then he goes back over the moors and pauses at Gimmerton Kirk, noting how it has decayed even in the past seven months. He thinks all is peaceful as he views the three graves, and that those buried there must be at rest: it is for the reader to decide whether this is true.

■ Self-test questions Chapters 29–34

Uncover the plot

Delete two of the three alternatives given, to find the correct plot. Beware possible misconceptions and muddles.

Linton/Heathcliff/Hareton arrives to fetch Nelly/Edgar/Cathy. He has seen Catherine's face/spirit/ghost: for 3/6/18 years he has felt/seen/rejected her spirit. Joseph/Zillah/Mary tells Nelly Linton/Heathcliff/Hareton has died. Cathy rebuffs Hareton's/Joseph's/Heathcliff's efforts to annoy/please/eject her. On the way to Gimmerton/London/the North, Lockwood/Nelly/Zillah sees her approval/contempt/help of his efforts to read/write/shoot. Returning, he finds life unchanged/changed/grim: Cathy and Hareton are ill/in love/fighting, Heathcliff away/injured/dead. Nelly tells how a repentant/devious/angry Cathy asked Hareton/Heathcliff/Joseph to forgive her: they fought/read/walked together, and were 'sworn enemies/allies/lovers'. After clearing the kitchen/garden/library, Cathy soothed/enraged/ignored and Hareton defended/fought/defied Heathcliff, who said he had no will for death/revenge/love, desiring only love/forgiveness/death. 'Wild and glad/stricken/sad', refusing to rest or eat/go out/talk, he died at the locked/broken/open window. At the graves, Lockwood can't imagine 'unquiet/restless/peaceful slumbers, for the ghosts/bodies/sleepers in that dark/quiet/green earth.'

Who? What? Where? Why? How?

1   Whom does Hareton remind Heathcliff of – and to what ironic effect?
2   Who will live at (a) Wuthering Heights and (b) the Grange after the end of the novel?
3   What events previously narrated by Isabella (17) are explained here?
4   What has tormented Heathcliff for eighteen years?
5   What is the last argument Cathy has with Heathcliff – and why is it the last?
6   When did Heathcliff open Catherine's grave, and what effect did it have on him?
7   Why does Cathy reject kindness from Hareton at first – and what changes her mind?
8   How has the scene at the Heights symbolically changed when Lockwood makes his fourth/final visit?
9   How does Heathcliff behave in the last days of his life?
10 How does Heathcliff want to be buried, and what arrangements has he already made?

Once upon a time...

1   What narrative voices do we hear in these chapters?
2   What is 'present time' in these chapters?
3   Where do Nelly's narratives of the past break into (a) further past and (b) future?
4   How many times has Lockwood visited the Heights altogether? Identify each.

Familiar themes

1   What part do books play in the developing relationship between Cathy and Hareton?
2   Give TWO examples of nature used symbolically in these chapters.
3   Quote a reference to Heathcliff as the 'devil' from Chapters 29 and 33. What do you notice about them?

Double dates

In these chapters, events move from past, to present, to present-become-past, to future. Now we can sort them into chronological order. What happened in the following months – and in what chapter?

1801: August, September, October, November, December.
1802: January, February, March, April, May, September.
1803: January

How to write a coursework essay

Most of you are probably studying *Wuthering Heights* as part of a Wide Reading coursework assignment for GCSE English/English Literature. If we look at the requirement of the NEAB examinations, we find that this assignment must involve *comparison* between a complete pre-twentieth-century prose text and a suitable twentieth-century text. It is also essential to make certain comments on the historical, social and cultural background to the texts. *Wuthering Heights* presents a view of society so different from the twentieth-century that this is not difficult to build into your essay. You might have already noted that this is something of a historical novel, being set some 50 years before the date of writing. In the following pages we examine three possible subjects for Wide Reading assignments. Throughout the **Text commentary** the **Essays icon** draws attention to useful material for these assignments.

There are, of course, some general principles for these assignments.

Comparison is essential. No credit is given for telling the story of all or part of *Wuthering Heights* and that of a twentieth-century story with a vaguely similar theme. It is essential that you show that, while Brontë's presentation of love or her narrative method has a certain effect, your twentieth-century author affects the reader totally differently, in the same or in a partially similar way.

Though comparison is essential, it is not required that you devote an equal amount of your essay to each of the texts. Similarly, there is no requirement that your twentieth-century comparative text is another novel: short stories, plays and poems are acceptable, and the only restriction is that the text 'must be of sufficient substance and quality to merit serious study'.

Your choice of twentieth-century comparative text is important. There must be *specific* grounds for comparison. This can, of course, mean that the twentieth-century story or novel is opposite in effect from Brontë: using similar ideas differently is a good ground for comparison, as too is obtaining comparable effects by different means.

The *most important consideration* in writing the essay is that it must develop an argument or explain a point of view consistently throughout. Choosing a title matters: if you write an essay called 'Love in *Wuthering Heights* and D.H. Lawrence's stories, you are not directing yourself towards a specific comparison. The comparison should be made throughout the essay, not necessarily in the same sentence, but at least in adjacent paragraphs. Careful advance planning will aid you in organising your theme or argument: making notes on the material, putting these notes in order, then working through two or three drafts of the essay. Thus you should be able to make a decision on what each paragraph is about, as far as possible signalling that to the reader in the opening sentence, often called a *topic sentence* because it states the topic of the paragraph.

In terms of length of essay, do bear in mind that it is only one of several pieces of coursework and there is no need for a 5,000 word blockbuster. Many essays will exceed 1,000 words: by how much depends on the material you wish to present and the advice of your teacher.

Narration

Give an account of the employment of multiple narrators in Wuthering Heights *and explain what effects are achieved by this. Compare this to the narrative method used in William Wharton's* Pride *and discuss how suitable each is to the material the author wishes to present.*

In this essay you have to 'explain', 'compare' and 'discuss', but first you must 'give an account' of a complicated method. At one time it was often claimed that Emily Brontë's narrative method was confused and confusing; nothing could be further from the truth. The **family trees** in the front of this guide show how precise is her chronology.

To explain Brontë's narrative method it is necessary to concentrate on two areas: the chronology and the choice of narrators. The novel does not use a conventional flash-back technique, beginning at the end of the story, but takes a more circuitous route: starting some 90 per cent of the way through, then telling the story so far, moving on to the very end and supplying the last stage in another flash-back. This enables events from different times to be placed side by side, as in the last chapter with Heathcliff's death, the appearance of the ghosts and the marriage of Cathy and Hareton.

Secondly, the choice of the narrators is crucial. Of the two main narrators, Lockwood provides a link between the 'civilised' world and the Heights and contributes mightily with his naiveté, vanity and misunderstandings. Nelly Dean, on the other hand, knows more of these people than anyone else (even Heathcliff talks to her quite naturally) and her slanting of events towards her own self-image warns the reader against taking things at face value. Brontë has a strict rule that all narration must be first-hand: Isabella is the most obvious 'minor' narrator, with a letter and a desperate spoken account, but characters from Heathcliff and Catherine to Zillah tell sections of the story as eye-witnesses: fortunately everyone talks to Nelly Dean!

With *Pride* we have a simpler, but still effective, method. It is the story of a lion, part of a Wall of Death act in New Jersey in the 1930s, which escapes, kills a man and has to be shot. Very much involved in this are his keeper, Cap

Modig, and a 10-year-old boy, Dickie Kettleson, who has befriended the lion. The narrative method alternates first-person accounts of Dickie's childhood with a historical perspective on the life of Sture Modig, World War One hero and champion race driver, fallen on hard times. At first the sections are lengthy and deal with quite different times and situations. Gradually, as they collide, the sections shorten and they become twin perspectives on the same events. (There is even an explanatory text-book section on the natural life-style of lions.)

You will need to explain, with effective use of examples, how these two methods suit the authors' intentions: both are highly effective, though the novels could hardly be more different. *Wuthering Heights* is one of the most vividly immediate of great nineteenth-century novels – the reader is present throughout – and one in which many of the characters are not clear-cut: Heathcliff, for instance, is presented equally dramatically as a devil and a romantically selfless lover. It is also a novel in which rapid change and re-change occur in a fairly short time-span, made apparently shorter by the narrative method, and in which Brontë concentrates on certain characters and events to the exclusion of others: it is obvious, for instance, that the older Lintons interest her not at all. All this is aided by the chosen method of narration.

In the case of *Pride* there is again an element of the multiple perspective of *Wuthering Heights*, but mainly the narration creates an effect of tragic convergence: two apparently different tales coming together. It is also a novel which starts from one final event, something that might be a story in a newspaper, and investigates (from a variety of angles) where it came from and what it led to.

This is a good example of texts comparable for one specific feature and your conclusion could simply summarise the methods and their effects.

Love and marriage

A major theme of Wuthering Heights *is that of choice (or lack of it) in love and marriage. Compare Emily Brontë's treatment of this theme with that of D.H. Lawrence in such stories as* Daughters of the Vicar.

There are many possible essay-titles on love, passion and marriage in Wuthering Heights and there is certainly no reason why you should not compare the passion of Catherine and Heathcliff with the central relationship in a twentieth-century romantic novel. There are, however, two provisos: your twentieth-century novel must pass the 'quality control' stipulation (check with your teacher) and your title must be precise and specific enough.

The title we are considering looks particularly at the specific question of choice in love and marriage. The amount of interesting and relevant material for this is enormous and writing a good essay should be fairly straightforward.

You should look at specific motives. Marriage for revenge and the desire to acquire wealth and property is something that Heathcliff does twice: once in his own person, once in the forced marriage of his son. There is some similarity with Catherine's choice of Edgar for his social graces and position, though she is far less calculating. Marriages for love are not always idealised. Hindley and Frances appear to love each other, but are presented as incurably trivial and Isabella's infatuation with Heathcliff is as childish as it is foolish. Even Edgar's lack of passion is occasionally subject to critical review.

Developing the above suggestions with suitable examples will provide a substantial body of relevant comment, but there are two areas which need specific emphasis. An examination of the differences between Catherine's love for Heathcliff (in which there is no choice) and for Edgar (a definite conscious choice) should start with Chapter 9 and contain detailed examinations of Chapters 11 and 15 among others. The final marriage (between Cathy and Hareton) could be described as the only one in which both choose wisely: you should examine the stages by which this choice comes about.

The settings of D.H. Lawrence's stories are, of course, different from the moors and the Heights, but many share, to some extent, the remoteness and the sense of people living close to harsh reality. Written in the early years of the twentieth century, the stories show a notable awareness of class which is also a key element of *Wuthering Heights*: Catherine would be ashamed of marriage to Heathcliff, whereas Edgar is totally suitable. Lawrence also, like Brontë, stresses the importance of independence of character and choice.

Though it is perfectly acceptable to focus on one story, you might find it easier to make reference to several Lawrence stories. One that offers comparable choices to *Wuthering Heights* is *Daughters of the Vicar*, a story of much less passion than Brontë's novel, but one that reflects the same elements of class, social rejection and independence of mind. In this case the choice is split between two sisters, daughters of the vicar of a Midlands mining community. One chooses the curate, a respectable choice, but a poor specimen of manhood; the other chooses a collier: each has her reasons. You can support this with several stories which similarly reflect the (usually unhappy) choices of love and marriage: Elizabeth Bates marrying 'beneath herself' in *Odour of Chrysanthemums*, scenes of unhappy marriage in *Strike Pay* or (more amusingly) the independent young women striking back in *Tickets, Please!*

The conclusion you draw is your own decision. You might summarise the various ways in which Brontë and Lawrence show the effects of social class or the failures of choice, or you might like to remind the reader that the power of *Wuthering Heights* depends to a great extent on a central relationship so strong that the whole concept of choice is irrelevant.

Place

Discuss the ways in which Emily Brontë utilises the sense of place to add reality and power to Wuthering Heights. *How do her methods resemble those of Graham Swift in* Waterland?

The power of images of place is similar in these two novels; the methods less so. The first obvious similarity is that both books are named after places, not characters: the farmhouse on the Yorkshire Moors and the Fen Country of East Anglia. It is almost as if the places are the main characters – and that is largely true. The second strong similarity is that both places are remote communities. This leads to the third great similarity: that the people in these areas are strange and distinct in their behaviour and attitudes. The wildness of the characters in *Wuthering Heights* is too much for Mr Lockwood; the inbreeding and clannishness of the marshes are similarly disturbing.

Both novels are powered by sex and secrets and adopt an unusual narrative method to emphasise this. In each case the reader is invited to share different time-periods simultaneously, with Nelly Dean telling Lockwood a story in which he occasionally participates, or Tom Crick delivering History lessons that turn into his own story.

Wuthering Heights uses a narrower range and greater intensity than *Waterland* in its presentation of place. There are two houses, each with identifiable, though changing, characteristics: at times, for instance, the Grange represents well-walled security, whilst the Heights is hell itself. You should have no trouble relating the houses to their inhabitants or charting the changing image of the Heights. You should equally find it straightforward to prove the powerful emotions associated with the Heights (Catherine's, especially) or the lure of the Moors to characters as different as Heathcliff and young Cathy.

The geographical centre of *Waterland* is more diffuse, from the town of Gildsey to the remote canal lock. The time period is wider: if the story centres on an event in World War Two, our understanding of the Fens requires the history of the locality from the seventeenth century. The methods of presenting place are similarly varied, with stories of apparently unrelated events in styles from history to reminiscence. Eventually the history of the Atkinsons of Gildsey and the traumatic events of Cricks, Parrs and Metcalfs in 1943 overlap in an East Anglian saga.

There is much detail needed to support the many similarities and differences in the use of place in the two novels. Perhaps the best conclusion is that both Emily Brontë and Graham Swift convince us that their stories could not have happened in the same way anywhere else.

How to write an examination essay

Though most of you will be required to write on *Wuthering Heights* as part of your coursework, some of you may need to answer an examination question on it. This section considers one specific title on the novel, but also gives general advice on how to approach an English Literature essay.

Wuthering Heights *deals with two main periods of time: up to 1784 and between 1800 and 1802. Compare the events and characters of the two halves of the novel. You should examine such features as:*
changes in Heathcliff and Edgar;
similarities and contrasts between the two generations of Lintons, Earnshaws and Heathcliffs;
similarities and contrasts between the pattern of events in each half.

Before you start writing

- The first essential is thorough revision. It is important that you realise that even Open Book examinations require close textual knowledge. You will have time to look up quotations and references, but *only if you know where to look.*

- Read the questions very carefully, both to choose the best one and to take note of exactly what you are asked to do.

- Do not answer the question you *imagine or hope* has been set. In the case of the title we are considering, you are not asked to tell the story of each half of the novel, though you are asked to make comparisons between key events. So, for instance, you will need to compare Catherine's need to escape to the moors with Cathy's rather more protected forays. One leads from the Heights to the Grange, the other the opposite. Each leads to a husband called Linton. You will also need to deal with such things as the denial of education to Heathcliff and Hareton. This is not the same as telling the story.

- Identify all the key words in the question that mention characters, events and themes, and instructions as to what to do, e.g. compare, contrast, comment, give an account, etc. Write a short list of the things you have to do. In this case 'compare', the key word, involves differences as well as similarities. You will need to chart the development of vengeance in Heathcliff and passiveness in Edgar, and to make such character comparisons as the two Catherines and their actual or potential husbands.

- Look at the points you have identified and jot down what you are going to say about each. For example, the character of Hareton recalls in different ways both Catherine and the young Heathcliff: you will need to consider how his situation reflects Heathcliff and how Heathcliff reacts to these recollections.

- Decide in what order you are going to deal with the main points. Number them in sequence. This is a matter of choice, but do not use chronological order: 'Heathcliff is brought to Wuthering Heights as a child by old Mr Earnshaw.' You may wish to follow the three main areas of the question in sequence, but do not forget to make comparisons within each area.

Writing the essay

- The first sentences are important. Try to summarise your response to the question so the examiner has some idea of how you plan to approach it. For example: 'The two generations in *Wuthering Heights* mirror each other to a considerable extent, but the corruption of Heathcliff's love into a thirst for vengeance casts a pall of fear until, as he tires of revenge, a new serenity enters the novel.' Jump straight into the essay; do not nibble at the edges for a page and a half. A personal response is rewarded, but you must always answer the question – as you write your essay, *refer back* to your list of points.

- Answer *all* of the question. Many students spend all their time answering just one part of a question and ignoring the rest. This prevents you gaining marks for the parts left out. In the same way, failing to answer enough questions on the examination is a waste of marks which can always be gained most easily at the start of an answer.

- There is no 'correct' length for an essay. What you must do is spend the full time usefully in answering all parts of the question (spending longer than the allotted time by more than a few minutes is dangerous). Some people write faster than others; they don't always get the best marks! It is an advantage if you can organise your time well enough to reach an elegant conclusion, but it is better to leave an essay without a conclusion than to fail to start the next question.

- Take care with presentation, spelling and punctuation. It is generally unwise to use slang or contractions (e.g. 'they've' for 'they have').

- Use quotation or paraphrase when it is relevant and contributes to the quality and clarity of your answer. References to events often do not need quotation, but the exact words of, for instance, Catherine's 'I *am* Heathcliff' speech is essential to our full understanding. *Extended* quotations are usually unhelpful and are often used as padding, which is a complete waste of time.

Self-test answers Chapters 1–7

Uncover the plot

Lockwood, tenant of Thrushcross Grange, visits Heathcliff, finding him inhospitable, and meets Mrs Heathcliff, scornful widow of Heathcliff's son, and Hareton Earnshaw: both seem hated by Heathcliff. Lockwood reads Catherine's diary of Hindley's cruelty and dreams of Catherine Linton's ghost. Mrs Dean says Heathcliff, found by Mr Earnshaw, was 'thick' with Catherine, but ill-treated by Hindley, who returned from college with Frances when Mr Earnshaw died. Heathcliff and Catherine ran wild: at the Grange, Catherine was injured and stayed. Attracted to the Lintons, she still felt for Heathcliff, unfairly punished by Hindley.

Who? What? When? Where? Why? How?

1   Heathcliff's or Hareton's wife: in fact, daughter of Catherine and Edgar Linton, widow of Heathcliff's son. A servant or Heathcliff's son: in fact, the dispossessed son of Hindley and Frances (2) (4)

2   Catherine Earnshaw/Heathcliff/Linton (3). The ghost he is about to meet was Catherine Earnshaw, then Linton – linked even in death to Heathcliff. The girl downstairs was Catherine Linton, then Heathcliff (married to his son) – and will marry Hareton to become another Catherine Earnshaw

3   Reaching out to stop the tree knocking on the window; grasping a hand; sawing its wrist on the broken glass; the ghost of Catherine Linton wailing to be let in after twenty years lost on the moors (3)

4   Caught peering through the Grange windows, Catherine is injured by the Lintons' dog: she is taken in, but Heathcliff is thrown out. She enters a new civilised world; he is the wild outsider still (6)

5   After the Lintons' first visit. Heathcliff was unfairly kept from the festivities, and humiliated in front of his 'rival' Edgar – just when he was making a real effort to 'be good' and daring to be cheerful (7)

6   He was found in Liverpool, of unknown (presumed gipsy) origins. He is a 'cuckoo', an outsider (4)

7   Heathcliff 'usurped' his privileges, and his father's affections; his father became an 'oppressor' on Heathcliff's behalf; he lost his 'last ally' when even Nelly softened towards Heathcliff (4)

8   Humiliated by Hindley's scorn, Heathcliff can't take a comment from Edgar about his long hair (7)

9   Catherine teaches him, and joins him constantly in the fields, where they plot revenge together (4)

10 'Trying to raise her self-respect with fine clothes and flattery', and 'separating the two friends'. (7)

Once upon a time...

1   Lockwood. Patronising and self-centred, draws wrong conclusions (mistakes dead rabbits for cats!), and attributes his own motives to others (e.g. emotional timidity to Heathcliff!) (1) (2) Our inability to rely on his 'instinct' and 'conjecture' forces us to be more objective in our response to events

2   Catherine Earnshaw; diary (3). Interest aroused by his one supporter, before less sympathetic views

3   Nelly Dean. Intimacy with families, domestic scene (4); 'steady, reasonable' and 'reflective' (7)

4   Heathcliff – telling Nelly (who is telling Lockwood!) about his and Catherine's 'visit' to Thrushcross (6)

5   Present: November1801. Lockwood's romance, that summer (1). Catherine's diary: Sunday soon after Mr Earnshaw's death (3). Nelly's long 'flashback' starting 1771 with Heathcliff's arrival and ending with his vow of vengeance, Christmas 1777 (4–7)

Familiar themes

1   'Mrs Heathcliff' in the house (2). Heathcliff in the garret (7). Catherine's ghost is locked out of the Heights (3). Hindley locks Heathcliff and Catherine out, the night they go to the Grange (6)

2   Dogs attack Lockwood, forcing him to stay at the Heights (2). The same happens to Catherine at the Grange (6). Heathcliff is like 'a vicious cur that appears to know the kicks it gets are its desert' (7)

3   Ghost appears at window (3). Heathcliff and Catherine look through Grange windows (6)

4   Fires are out (2); a 'huge, warm, cheerful apartment' with 'an immense fire' (2). The Grange is 'beautiful – a splendid place': heaven to Heathcliff and Cathy looking through the window (6)

5   Snow storm, wind. Rattle of fir-bough against window is central to Lockwood's dream: also, disturbing atmosphere – and weather echoes the stormy passions of Catherine and Heathcliff (3)

A capital fellow?

1   Dark gipsy look v 'homely', ordinary. Gentlemanly v rustic. Inhospitable v cheerful, welcoming (1)

2   Her diary suggests closeness. Heathcliff begs ghost – 'my heart's darling' – to come in 'at last' (3)

3   Conflict: wife grumbles; children lose presents; Catherine punished for reacting; Nelly sent away (4)

4   Dark 'as if it came from the devil'; 'imp of Satan' (4); eyes like a 'couple of black fiends' (7): strange influence; cursing; hate and revenge; surrounded by dogs. 'Gift of God' (4); innocent view of heaven when Mr Earnshaw dies (5); first view of him as gentleman landlord (1); Catherine's love (3)

5   Heathcliff taller, broader, stronger, braver. Edgar handsome, fair, well-dressed/behaved, rich (7)

■ Self-test answers Chapters 8–12

Uncover the Plot

Hareton is born: Frances dies: Hindley grows 'desperate'. Heathcliff has deteriorated, but saves Hareton's life. Hearing Cathy say she loves Edgar, he leaves before she says she loves him. Catherine catches fever. She marries Edgar. The Lintons humour her, and they are happy. Heathcliff returns: Catherine is excited – and scornful because Edgar is upset. Heathcliff moves into the Heights, and gambles with Hindley. Isabella is infatuated with Heathcliff, despite warnings from Catherine: Heathcliff is contemptuous, but attracted by her inheritance. Catherine and Heathcliff argue: Edgar finally confronts them, and Catherine falls ill. Kenneth prescribes quiet – but Mary brings news that Heathcliff and Isabella have eloped.

Who? What? Why? How?

1   (a) Catherine tells Heathcliff (10), (b) Nelly tells Edgar (11), (c) Kenneth tells Nelly, Mary tells Edgar (12)

2   Hindley: especially after Catherine blames him for degrading Heathcliff so she can't marry him (9). Catherine – treated him 'infernally' (11)
3   'Infernal' – the servants leave, 'decent' people avoid it, Hindley drinks, gambles and is a tyrant (8)
4   Awaiting Heathcliff in storm; turmoil, guilt (9). Choice between Edgar and Heathcliff, self-neglect (11)
5   He is 'nameless'; would be Edgar's heir; his mind 'revolts' Edgar (10). He is a 'moral poison' (11)
6   'No temptation to show her rough side' with Lintons, no encouragement to be polite at home; tries to be friends with Edgar and Heathcliff. Having argued with Heathcliff, is enraged in Edgar's presence, slaps him (9)
7   Hears Cathy say she loves Edgar: degrading to marry Heathcliff. He misses her saying she loves him (9)
8   Lost benefit and love of learning, and sense of superiority; acquired 'ignoble look', moroseness (8)
9   She 'loves' him; Heathcliff does not know what love is; Linton's money will help Heathcliff (9)
10 Tall, athletic, upright; face decisive, intelligent; dignified, not rough. Still 'half-civilised ferocity' (10)

Once upon a time...
1   Later the night Nelly started her story (the third day of 'present time'!) (9) Four weeks later (10). The reminder that Heathcliff is 'now' a landlord and gentleman brings us down to earth.
2   (8) starts the summer after the Christmas in (7). After the storm in (9), we skip three years to Catherine's marriage: April 1783 (10). Resumes in September that year, with Heathcliff's return
3   Joseph reports the gambling and drinking at the Heights (10). Mary reports Isabella's elopment (12)
4   Can't understand other-worldly passions (9), yet superstitious (9,11). Biased towards Edgar (10) and even Hindley (11). Misjudges Edgar's reactions and Catherine's illness (11,12)
5   Relives childhood. Foresees death and burial. Recalls her bed, and the fir at her window (12)

Familiar themes
1   Cathy locks Edgar in with Heathcliff (11), and herself in her room (12). Edgar is 'unable' to leave Cathy (8)
2   Dreams leaving heaven for heath (9). Would 'be herself' again on the hills (12). Forsees grave 'in the open air' (12). Only indoors with Edgar is she 'wondrously peaceful' (10). The elements cause her fever (9).
3   (a) He appeared 'possessed of something diabolical' – but Hindley's treatment was 'evil' (8). (b) She says his 'bliss' lies, like Satan's, in 'inflicting misery' – but she has at least partly made him what he is (11)
4   When Catherine is found ill (9) and is ill again (11): her self-destructive freedom

What's love got to do with it?
1   Edgar (9), Isabella (10): Lintons contrast with passion, love and hate of Earnshaws and Heathcliff
2   He is handsome, pleasant, young, cheerful, rich and loves her (9)
3   'Because he's more myself than I am. Whatever our souls are made of, his and mine are the same' (9)
4   For Edgar: foliage – 'time will change it… as winter changes the trees.' For Heathcliff: 'the eternal rocks beneath – a source of little visible delight, but necessary' (9)

5 Hindley's 'wild-beast's fondness' for Hareton, summed up in the command: 'Damn thee, kiss me!' (9)

Life cycle
Hareton is born; Frances dies (8). Hareton is saved; Nelly sings of a dead woman's child; Catherine falls ill; Mr and Mrs Linton catch fever and die; Catherine marries Edgar (9). Heathcliff disrupts the marriage (10). Nelly recalls child Hindley; Heathcliff steals Hareton's filial love and disrupts the Linton family; Catherine falls ill again (11). Catherine relives childhood, foresees death; Isabella and Heathcliff elope; Edgar disowns his sister (12)

◼ Self-test answers Chapters 13–20

Uncover the plot
Isabella tells Nelly about her arrival at the Heights: only the dog was kind. Heathcliff shows cruelty to Isabella and forces Nelly to let him see Catherine. Violently holding each other – tormented by thoughts of her death – they forgive each other. Catherine dies after Cathy is born. Heathcliff cries: 'I cannot live without my soul!' Isabella plots with Hindley against him, and flees to London. Hindley dies soon after: Nelly is grieved; Heathcliff is master of the Heights. Edgar fetches Linton from a dying Isabella. Cathy discovers the Heights, meets Hareton and won't accept he is her cousin. She makes a 'pet' of Linton, but he is claimed by Heathcliff, who plans to make him a gentleman, as an instrument of revenge.

Who? What? Where? Why? How?
1 She says Edgar and Heathcliff broke her heart. He says she broke her own heart – and so his (15)
2 (a) His sister Isabella tormented (14), her son Linton controlled (20) and his property – with Heathcliff as heir (16). (b) His son impoverished and his property, taken over (17)
3 She is pregnant: a male heir would secure the Grange from 'a stranger's gripe' (13). Heathcliff – the outsider – inherits.
4 Heathcliff calls him 'property', despises him, hates him for 'memories he revives'. But must keep him alive to inherit, wants to 'preserve the superior and the gentleman in him' to degrade the Lintons (20)
5 Not with the Lintons, but in the open (17). She prophesied this (12) – and it unites her with Heathcliff
6 Blames him for Catherine's illness (13) Nelly blames Catherine (14). She blames Heathcliff and Edgar (15)
7 Wants the chance to win back the money he has lost to him, for Hareton's sake (13)
8 Likes Hareton instinctively, but he is 'degrading' as a cousin (18). Makes a 'pet' of Linton (19). She relives her mother's dilemma: Cathy too will marry the 'wrong' one – but has the chance to put it right
9 (a) Defiant, violently stricken; curses her to haunt rather than leave him, seeks revenge. (b) Distracted, then resigned: remembers, hopes in heaven, channels his love to their child (17)
10 Locks him out; scorns his grief; blames him for Catherine's death; says Catherine would have hated 'the degrading title of Mrs Heathcliff'. To 'taste the delight of paying wrong for wrong' (17)

Once upon a time…

1   Isabella. Her letter's cultured style gives full weight to the Heights' strangeness (13). The tale of her escape allows an eye-witness account, and emphasises her moral deterioration (17)

2   Nelly breaks off (end 14): a brief respite – and allows Lockwood's trite response. Nelly lets Lockwood 'judge… those things' (17): 'at least, you'll think you will' shows the vanity of moral judgements

3   Chapter 18, after Hindley dies. Space for the next generation of the families to come into play

Familiar themes

1   Heathcliff locks his door against Hindley (13). Hindley and Isabella lock Heathcliff out (17). Isabella is a prisoner and Nelly is threatened with it (14). Linton becomes a prisoner (20). Wuthering Heights

2   She says she hates him, but 'can dimly imagine that I could still be loving him, if –' (17)

3   Seized his hair, wrenching, grinding, impressions left blue, branded, writhe, gnashed, frantic (15)

4   Imagining Edgar's love could satisfy Catherine is like planting an oak in a flower-pot, or containing the sea in a horse-trough. Echo of Catherine's comparison of 'foliage' love and 'eternal rocks' love (9)

Till death do us part?

1   Asks him to imagine outliving her; says he will forget her and be happy again (15)

2   Sharing torment, but then: 'I shall love [him] yet, and take him with me – he's in my soul.' (15)

3   Heathcliff cries: 'May you not rest, as long as I am living!… Haunt me then! Be with me always' (17)

4   Locks of hair entwined in her locket. Grave in Heathcliff's world, yet joined by Edgar (16)

5   Remembers her 'with ardent, tender love'; aspires to join her; has 'a connection with her' in Cathy (18)

■ Self-test answers Chapters 21–28

Uncover the plot

Cathy and Nelly, meeting Heathcliff on the moor, visit the Heights. Linton, weak but graceful, joins Cathy in mocking Hareton. Edgar warns that Heathcliff is a 'diabolical man', but Cathy exchanges letters with Linton: Nelly burns them. Heathcliff tells her Linton is dying of a broken heart: Cathy secretly visits him when Nelly is ill. They fight with Hareton, argue – then reconcile. Nelly tells Edgar: Cathy is forbidden to visit again. Linton writes to Edgar, asking to see Cathy. They meet near the Heights – Linton is apathetic – and again, when Edgar is dying: Cathy is impatient, Linton terrified. Taking him home, Cathy and Nelly are imprisoned by Heathcliff, who forces Cathy to marry Linton. Nelly, freed by Zillah, runs to Edgar. Cathy escapes: her father dies.

Who? What? Where? Why? How?

1   Hareton. He is like Heathcliff – 'no fool', strong and wild – and suffers the same treatment he did (21)

2   (a) Spoilt, demanding, self-pitying, weak, perverse, childish, spiteful (23). (b) A harder self-centredness: wants to punish Cathy, be master of the Grange, have all Cathy's things (28)
3   Write love letters to Cathy (21) and uncomplaining letters to Edgar (25). To meet Cathy on the moors (25). He is terrorised by Heathcliff and is told his only escape is with Cathy to the Grange (27)
4   Edgar disapproved of Isabella's marriage. So she won't tell Edgar about her visits – but it fails (21)
5   'Not bad natured' (21), 'no fool', makes an effort for Cathy (24). He says 'I'd have loved the lad had he been someone else' – but rejoices even more to have ruined 'first-rate qualities' in Hindley's son (21)
6   Outside the protective wall of the Grange (22). On the moors – but too close to the Heights (26, 27)
7   It would bring the Linton inheritance within his control without possibility of 'disputes' (23)
8   Controls Linton's letters (21); gets her to visit by saying Linton is dying for her and needs her kindness – and 'blackmailing' her with her love letters (22). Threatens to hold her till Edgar is dead (27)
9   She finds him graceful and pretty: a 'pet' (21). Is troubled by his 'selfishness and spite' but pities his sufferings (24). Is irritated by his lack of interest (26). Is exasperated at his demands, when Edgar is ill – and finally recognises him as the 'abject reptile' and cowardly traitor he is (27)
10 Tries to change his will, so Catherine's personal fortune is not part of Heathcliff's inheritance. The lawyer comes too late – already 'bought' by Heathcliff (28)

Once upon a time…
1   Ill for 3 weeks: Catherine tells her story (24). Imprisoned for 5 days: Zillah fills her in (28)
2   Mar 1800, Nov 1800, Mar 1801, Aug 1801. Time accelerating towards 'present'.
3   Illnesses remind us of his situation; Nelly reminds us of his attraction to Cathy (25). Nelly's story is almost up to date, and Lockwood must take over his 'real-time' narration (in chapter 30).

Familiar themes
1   Edgar: accelerating Heathcliff's plans (22). Linton: accelerating his plans, and showing their brutality (22). Nelly – allowing Cathy to meet Linton (23). Lockwood (still!): to account for passive role as audience
2   Cathy lends Linton books (21). Cathy bribes the groom with books (24). Hareton kicks Cathy's book out (24). Hareton learns to read the inscription: his birthright, if he only knew its significance (24)
3   Linton wants 'all to lie in an ecstasy of peace'; Cathy wants 'all to sparkle and dance in a glorious jubilee' (24)
4   (a) Spring: her last unclouded time for a while (21) Autumn: the onset of a long dark period (22)
5   She pities him, wants to 'direct him', 'look after him', 'make a pet of him'. He taunts her that her mother loved his father (23); later, they find Heathcliff's and Cathy's toys (24)
6   Although worried about leaving Cathy, he longs to join Catherine (25). We already know he is buried beside her (16), where Heathcliff, with an even more intense longing, will join them (34)

Parallel lines

1 Cathy and her 'pretty Linton' taunt Hareton, for his illiteracy, country accent and boorish behaviour (21)
2 Hareton locks Cathy and Linton out: Linton shrieks 'If you don't let me in I'll kill you!' (24)
3 Nelly doesn't tell Edgar about the letters (21), but goes immediately to tell him of the secret visits (24).
4 Cathy escapes from the same room in the Heights to the Grange, via the lattice and fir (28)

■ Self-test answers Chapters 29–34

Uncover the plot

Heathcliff arrives to fetch Cathy. He has seen Catherine's face: for 18 years he has felt her spirit. Zillah tells Nelly Linton has died. Cathy rebuffs Hareton's efforts to please her. On the way to London, Lockwood sees her contempt of his efforts to read. Returning, he finds life changed: Cathy and Hareton are in love, Heathcliff dead. Nelly tells how a repentant Cathy asked Hareton to forgive her: they read together, and were 'sworn allies'. After clearing the garden, Cathy enraged and Hareton defended Heathcliff, who said he had no will for revenge, desiring only death. 'Wild and glad', refusing to rest or eat, he died at the open window. At the graves, Lockwood can't imagine 'unquiet slumbers, for the sleepers in that quiet earth.'

Who? What? Where? Why? How?

1 Catherine (31). He also seems a 'personification' of Heathcliff's youth (33). Revenge 'spoiled': he has gained the power, lost the will: he is the one tormented, by the presence of his 'victims' (33)
2 (a) Joseph and a lad (using only the kitchen). (b) Cathy and Hareton with Nelly (34)
3 Heathcliff's desperation when locked out, and his grief the following morning (29)
4 Hope of seeing Catherine at the Heights: he feels her there, expects to see her, never does (29)
5 He is angry about garden; she says he's taken their land/property, tries to set Hareton against him. Hareton asks her not to speak ill to/of him again: she never does – and Heathcliff is now past hate (33)
6 Evening of her burial: hopeful – then frustrated, anguished. Night of Edgar's burial: 'pacified a little' (29)
7 When she needed a friend, he wasn't there. She is sorry she crushed his desire to improve himself (30)
8 Gate unlocked, doors and lattices open; flowers in the garden; occupants reading, at peace (32)
9 Excited, joyful; goes out alone; doesn't eat or rest; seems distracted, smiling at an invisible presence; paces and talks to Catherine; talks of wills, funerals, heaven; locks himself away alone (34)
10 Evening; no prayers. Buried next to Catherine, walls separating them removed (29, 34)

Once upon a time...
1   Nelly (29), (32-34). Zillah (30). Heathcliff (29). Lockwood (31), (32), (34)
2   Jan 1802: story up-to-date, Lockwood leaves. (31). Sep 1802: he returns, hears the latest (32)
3   (a) Nelly and Heathcliff recall events 18 years ago (30). (b) Nelly anticipates the marriage (32)
4   First visit November 1801 (1). Second visit the following day – sees ghost (2). Third visit, after illness, to give notice Jan 1802 (31). Fourth visit, following September: all changed (32).

Familiar themes
1   He fetches for her – but she won't read to him (30). She says he stole her books from spite (actually trying to learn to please her) and 'debased' them: he burns them (31). She repents, reads aloud, coaxes him to read (32). Book gift is token of reconciliation (32). They grow close as she teaches him to read (33)
2   The moors 'In winter, nothing more dreary, in summer, nothing more divine' – like life at the Heights (32). Cathy and Hareton plant flowers from the Grange: 'seeds' of civilisation and joy at the Heights (33)
3   Cathy: he is 'lonely, like the devil, and envious like him' (29). Hareton: 'If he were the devil,... he would stand by him' (33). More sympathetic view: Heathcliff has suffered, and has been loved

Double dates

1801	1802	1802
Aug: Linton marries Cathy (27)	Jan: Lockwood leaves (31)	Sep: Lockwood returns (32)
Sep: Edgar dies (28)	Feb: Nelly returns to WH (32)	
Oct: Linton dies (30)	Mar: Hareton's accident (32)	1803
Nov: Lockwood arrives (1)	Apr: Cathy/Hareton read (34)	Jan: Cathy/Hareton marry (34)
Dec: Lockwood is ill (4)	May: Heathcliff dies (34)	